Finding My
Possibilities

Finding My Possibilities

Tracey R. Kern

CONSCIOUS SHIFT PUBLISHING

Florida

CSP

Published by Conscious Shift Publication

Conscious Shift Publishing Registered Offices: Saint Petersburg, FL 33710

Copyright 2016

Library of Congress Cataloging-in-Publications Data

Tracey R. Kern

Finding My Possibility/Tracey R. Kern

ISBN: 0997955201

ISBN 9780997955200

Published in the United States of America

Book design by Ellen Kaltenbacher

Dedication

To my beautiful wife, Andrea

Thank you for keeping our divine appointment. You have always allowed me to be me and for that I am forever grateful. Thank you for Consciously Shifting with me every day and making it fun even when it's not. You are the music I hear in silence and the light I see in darkness, you are my Moonbeam Baby.

I would like to extend a special thanks to my amazing editors, Mary Watson and Mary Dado. Without your nurturing help and magical touch, this book would not have been possible.

To all the beautiful messengers who have shown up and shared the journey with me, and there are so many...thank you. Thank you for venturing down the rabbit hole of possibility with me.

Table of Contents

Prologue

They say the only thing in life that's guaranteed is death and taxes. I disagree. The only thing in life that's guaranteed is change. Change is all there is, it governs everything, the change in seasons, the calendar months, hair growth, grocery shopping and let's not forget the caterpillar.

The caterpillar is an artist at mastering change; it starts out as a colorless little worm and turns into a wondrous flying piece of art. Beautiful and amazing, the caterpillar embraces change and the process of change for it knows that the outcome will be great.

Change is everything and for most of my life I lived in fear of change. To me, change represented chaos and uncertainty. Change meant I had to learn a new way to survive. I felt paralyzed by the thought of change and cloaked in fear by the "shoulds" and "should nots" imposed by the mere thought of change. This fear of change started as a child and eventually became engrained in my cellular memory as an adult. I perceived change as the enemy. It was outside of my understanding and anything outside of my understanding was the enemy.

I find it interesting that change is the basis for living and yet it was so utterly terrifying to me. I would create the most elaborate situations that would bring enormous and debilitating change in an effort to avoid the very change I was creating. I lived in and created unconscious change in an effort to find clarity. I lived life without taking responsibility for my actions, but blamed others while perceiving myself an innocent bystander of my own creation. I was pulled by the ebb and flow of life's currents, that to me, represented chaos and panic. I was a victim of my own doing and lived accordingly.

As I got older and survived my creations of change, I begin to understand that there was magic in change. At the calming of each chaotic episode I began to see that the only thing in life was change; change without waiting for the next shoe to drop. I began to understand that without change we go nowhere, we become stuck and unconscious, or as a teacher of mine use to say "S.O.S." He would say, "Watch out for stuck on stupid, it will lead you to living damn near dead." Something about that statement resonated with me and I began to look at change differently. I started to see the importance of change and learned how to consciously embrace it instead of fearing it. I began to gently shift into change instead of experiencing it through self-induced chaos or from a place of "S.O.S.".

That's how my story starts, by letting go of fear and getting unstuck. It's important to know the only difference between me and anyone else is that I chose to consciously and purposefully let go of the "S.O.S.". I chose to thrive in the face of change by embracing the beautiful shifts in consciousness change can bring. I chose to see what was possible while embracing the next adventure down that rabbit hole of possibility with a joyful heart. To strive and accept change with a smile on my face, knowing that great things are around every corner if I choose to look at it that way.

It is because of my shift in consciousness about change that I am now able to understand the purpose of change; change is the ambassador of possibility. This possibility shows up when it is time to move forward with your life's purpose. Bless these changes or shifts for they hold the opportunities you seek. Understand that change is what you have been asking for. Be aware and alert when coming upon an ending because it's easy to get stuck in the past and forget to live in the possibility of the new beginning that change is bringing. Trust and know it's all connected, it's purposeful, and like the finely constructed web of quantum possibility, it is why you chose to be here.

Chapter One

New Beginnings

What is it about family that can rock you to your core? I used to think that people and their "mommy issues" or "family dramas" were annoying. I wanted to hear nothing about it and felt that people needed to take responsibility for their own lives and just get over it. I had little if any tolerance for those who needed to, as I called it, "get a grip". That is until my own mommy/family issues could no longer be buried.

I was on my way to my father's funeral. My dad (whom I always called Fred) had just transitioned and was off to his next adventure. And while I understand that death is normally perceived as a sad occasion I couldn't help but be happy. Fred was now able to journey as he pleased. The nomad in him was free to roam, released from the constraints of life's shoulds and should nots. In addition to his new freedom, he no longer felt pain or suffering from the years of self-abuse and body neglect. He was free in every way and I felt this joyous freedom on his behalf. To me it was a celebration, however, I knew I was not going to a party nor was this feeling shared by the rest of his family. Fred's family consisted of my stepmother Linda, and a half-brother and half-sister who were not seeing or feeling the blessing in this at all. They were still grieving and experiencing the pain of watching him suffer in the hospital for nearly a month.

Upon arriving at the airport in Michigan I was greeted by my stepmother and half- sister. They were sad yet po-lite while giving the appearance that all was well, while filling me in on the details about the funeral. We discussed the viewing, the ceremony, how Fred would be buried in their family crypt, and about the full military honors that would be given at the gravesite; as well as the fact that the funeral home insisted on us riding in a limo to and from the cemetery. We laughed about how when Fred and Linda purchased the crypt, Fred's only request was that he be on top. Unfortunately, once you are placed in the crypt there is no pulling you out, so Fred would have to be okay with being on the bottom this time around. I was totally agreeable to all and I think they were actually sur-prised. I had to remember they didn't know me any more than I knew them and they had no reason to think I would be easy to deal with during this difficult situation. Over the years there had never been a relationship other than a po-lite phone call on holidays or the occasional birthday card, and if it were not for Fred's funeral we would not be communicating now. All we had was our Fred connection and the many years that were filled with preconceived notions and misunderstandings. Until right then we never saw or had a reason to correct or change our beliefs. There was never a compelling reason to cultivate a relationship of any kind. It was only now that we were forced to communicate and get along for this auspicious occasion that only Fred could have arranged.

The reason I did not have a relationship with Fred's wife or his children started when I was very young and was solidified at the age of eight when my mother and stepfather moved to Florida. I had only visited Fred or members of his family a few times in my life and now we had to all get along like a family. Driving from the airport you could feel the disease. For me, the only thing about this trip that was not uncomfortable was that I would see my cousins and aunts. That and a phone conversation I had with my cousin a few days earlier helped me feel a bit more at ease and know that someone understood the disconnect I was feeling.

I remember the conversation clearly, like it was just a moment ago. My cousin and I were discussing how bad Fred had gotten. I felt he should have been in hospice instead of having his body connected to machines and pumped full of drugs in an intensive care unit. We were discussing how she was going to the hospital that day to say good-bye. I asked her to tell Fred that I loved him and tell him it was okay, he and I were complete, and it was time for his next journey. She then said, and I will never forget it, "I just love how our family is there for each other, how we pull together and support each other". When I heard her words I felt the most powerful and debilitating rage followed by a pain pulsating through my body. I blurted out in a most sarcastic manner, "REALLY? I'm glad that's your experience, but I don't know the family you are speaking of. That has never been my experience. As a matter of fact, I have always felt like the kid who fell between the cracks, the one who no one ever had time for or even cared if they did have time." I believe I shocked her. Or maybe it was the way I went on for about ten minutes. Either way, she got an earful.

moved to be near the water and has made a career out of being creative.

My dad, Fred, was the sixth of eight children and grew up on a dairy farm. Now life on a farm is work, but a dairy farm redefines the concept of work. On a dairy farm things have to go on every day and I mean every day. There is no sick time or down time. The word vacation does not exist because cows have to be taken care of regardless of what season it is and whether or not you're tired. Every morning before school there was at least two hours of work to do, then each afternoon the same. I remember Fred talking about how hard the old man, my grandfather, was. Fred was a tender-hearted guy and when he told stories about growing up it never sounded like fun, until he talked about his mother, my grandmother Anna. Anna was kind and sweet, always baking and taking care of everyone or playing cards, her favorite pastime. I believe it was Anna's influence that made Fred so compassionate and the old man's temperament that made him so distant from others for most of his life.

I didn't get much of an opportunity to know my paternal grandmother, as she died when I was six. The memories I do have of her are filled with sweetness and love. She was always happy to see me and loved my dad; she called him Freddy and was always hugging and kissing on me. I remember this because no one else loved on me like she did. When she loved on you, you felt it and knew it was real. I remember it made me uncomfortable because no one I knew did that and I was afraid of her affection. I thought if she kissed on me I would get high blood pressure. Silly, I know.

◆ ◆ ◆

Back to Fred and Mom. They met at a high school football game. The actual year is sketchy but I think it was my mom's junior year in school. Fred was a good-looking farm boy from a smaller town about forty-five minutes away from where she lived. It was his good looks and convertible that got her attention. She was a sucker for a convertible. Their meeting and dating caused a bit of a stir too. Apparently both of them had "Kern" my dad's surname, in their family. Once they figured out they were not from the same family they were clear to date. Before long Fred was drafted, in boot camp, and then they married. Immediately after their wedding Fred was shipped out to Vietnam.

While in Vietnam they exchanged love letters and Fred sent home reel-to-reel movies to document the events he was experiencing. War was quite different from farm life and very strange compared to the small town he was used to. When Fred came back from Vietnam he was different. Being in war is hard and it changes you. But, for someone with a simple and loving soul who lived in a rural community, it was even more difficult. From this point on there was not a lot of connection between Mom and Fred, he was trying to cope and she got pregnant in hopes of keeping her husband and making it better. They started out young and naïve and then they had a whole new set of baggage filled with un-communicated expectations and emotions. As a result, there was a lot of drinking and cheating, a lot of pain and mystery. And then there was me.

Chapter Three

Things Shifted

It was 1974 and seven years into a problematic marriage and parenthood. Things were bad and getting worse. It was summer time and everything was coming to a head. Fred was in and out and Mom was now stuck with a three-year-old. Fred longed for a more adventurous life. He was willing to try new things and go places. He wanted to partner swap with local swingers, travel and be free. He had seen the world and was now back in a small town that no longer fit the new version of who he longed to be.

My mother's mom was no help and her father died before I was born from dementia, hard work and old age. Feeling stressed and hopeless my mom packed me up and headed north for a weekend.

We landed in a place called Sleeping Bear Dunes. For years I thought it was a bunch of sand dunes in the middle of the state. In fact, it's actually a beach off one of the

Great Lakes in Michigan. I even have videos of us there. This was her great escape from all the troubles and issues that were heavy on her heart.

She and Fred were not getting along and a few weeks earlier she had been in a car accident. She was following Fred in her VW Bug while he was out with his drinking friends and girlfriends. As she raced down the country back roads in an effort to keep up, she flipped the car. They knew she had been following them, but no one stopped, no one looked back; she was just there like an upside down turtle spinning. Luckily, she was not hurt, only minor scrapes to her body and a seriously bruised ego.

This lakeside weekend offered the solace she needed. A place to let it all go for a moment and just be. However, that's not how it went. Halfway through the weekend I remember her crying and begging for help asking, "What am I going to do, how am I going to do this? Please help me."

At the age of three this kind of thing is disturbing. No dad, no nurturing, you're a mess, and now you need help? I'm three. What am I supposed to do? What is my role in all of this? What do you want from me? I'm the kid here! I don't want to hear this!!! I don't remember anything else about that weekend or seeing my parents together again after that.

What I do remember are the stories of what followed before they were divorced.

I remember conversations about my father's infidelity and lack of concern for us. That there would be footprints on the roof of my mother's car from his girlfriend and that ultimately he was leaving her. He had found someone who was thin and beautiful. Something my mother was not...thin. Beautiful, maybe, thin no.

The events that took place during this time were pivotal in my life. I rarely if ever spent time with Fred anymore and there was little if any contact with his side of the family. During this time Fred was checking out everywhere in life. He evolved into fall-down-drunk-status and stayed there for every weekend, holiday and opportunity that presented itself. I know this because I saw him fall down on several occasions from being drunk. He spent little if any time with his family and definitely didn't spend time with me on our visitation weekends. I remember being picked up by his new wife every other Friday and spending most of the weekend with just her because he was out drinking and partying. My stepmother, Linda wanted little to do with me. I don't understand a lot about how their relationship worked except she put up with a lot of shit from him. He was really messed up for years and I think one of the things he loved about her was her family.

Her family was from the city and completely different from how he grew up. They were more than just city people; they were drunks and a few were criminals. On weekends and most days, they would sit on their front porch drinking and raising hell. The kids would go around stealing air caps off of people's car tires then flattening the tires just because. In addition to being perpetually drunk, Fred and his new father- and brothers-in-law went out and slept with whomever came along.

Weekends with Linda, my stepmother's family, were about which one of her brothers or sister, could torture and tease me until I cried. Even on weekends when I saw Fred we spent our time camping with Linda's family outside of Travers City in Michigan. Those weekends consisted of stealing people's four wheelers and bees flying up my shirt as I walked through the woods. That part is actually kind of funny. For years I had dreams of walking through school without a shirt on because I was afraid of bees flying up my sleeve.

Eventually, Fred and his new wife had a child. When this happened things changed. Now, like I said before, Linda wanted nothing to do with me and with the new baby I was even more in the way. Over time she lost what little patience she had with me because according to her, I was jealous of the new baby.

During this time there was an angel in my life named Dorothy. She lived next to my mother and me with her husband Charlie. Charlie gardened in a big way, flowers galore, vegetables everywhere, and his favorite, roses. Rose bushes framed in lilacs were everywhere. In his basement I remember he hung the flowers to be dried for fall bouquets. Towards the end of lilac season, he and I negotiated a clean-up fee. He paid me a dollar to pick up the lilacs that had fallen just to be kind and to give me something to do. His wife, Dorothy, baked and sewed like no tomorrow. She made fresh pies and cookies and always had a quilt project going. When I came home from the hospital I was actually wrapped in one of her quilting projects. I still have it today and cover up in it when I take naps; it is blue satin. At one time, it had white fringe. Charlie and Dorothy were kind and generous and offered a soothing comfort to my life that did not exist anywhere else. When I think about having grandparents in my life I think of them. I know they were the first in a long line of beautiful angels who showed up to watch over me on my journey.

Chapter Four

Ron and Mom

My mom met Ron in the spring of 1974 on one of her ventures into the dating world. Ron was too skinny and had knobby knees. He had jet-black hair and when he grew a beard it was fire red. He was an auto body specialist and had a very successful business with his brother. My mother met him at a Parents Without Partners meeting where he showed up drunk. She was very overweight and self-conscious; going to the meeting was a big step for her. She and Ron connected and she gave him her number. Weeks went by before she heard from him and when he called his first line was "I don't know where I got your number but would you like to go out with me?" As she was hanging up on him she heard him yell, "Wait...I'm joking!" After a long conversation they had their first date.

Ron drove a big red convertible and like his car, he was flashy and larger than life. He was fun and enjoyed having me come along on their adventures. For the moment,

into the car until I put the ring on and not be afraid of it. I stood in front of the car door for what seemed like hours and then Ron drove off. All I could do was cry and worry about how I would get back home. We were so far away and I didn't know the way. He eventually came back and I put the ring on and he let me in the car. My mom looked at me in the back seat and said, "That wasn't so bad was it?". We went to the movie and home. We never talked about it again and it was never again spoken of. This was the first time I experienced the wrath of Ron.

A few months later our town put on an end of summer, welcome to fall, type parade that went through the center of our small town. It was the highlight of the season and it showcased the local tractor companies and of course the high school football team. The town was abuzz. I remember it specifically because some of my big deal older friends were in the parade, specifically Lisa, the granddaughter of my angelic neighbors Dorothy and Charlie. Lisa was a cheerleader and rode in the fire truck that followed the tractors and Future Farmers of America (FFA) float; she was cute and I just loved seeing her. I remember smiling ear-to-ear for the rest of the afternoon. Later that evening when we got home I was told I could have some ice cream and to get it out of the freezer. I thought "Really?" Okay, I can do that. So I climbed up on a stool to reach the freezer and then the cupboard for my bowl.

I carefully opened the ice cream, blueberry cheesecake, from Moonies and proceeded to take a five-year-old's version of a serving of ice cream. I filled my bowl and then added more for good measure. It was heavenly. I was floating on blueberry sunshine and I felt high. Moments later, I hear Ron screaming at me while he called me a pig. He then continued to tell me I was stupid because I did not need that much ice cream and only fat pigs ate that much ice cream. In that moment I froze and then cried, I honestly didn't know what was going to happen next. Then I thought I really didn't understand the problem, I'm five and you just gave me the keys to ice cream heaven. You gave me permission to scoop away and then call me a pig and stupid? This was becoming par for the course in the new version of life according to Mom and Ron. Passive aggression served with a side of cruelty. Needless to say I didn't get to eat my blueberry cheesecake sunshine that day and I never got my own serving of ice cream again.

Things were beginning to look different and unravel because I could see that Mom was now feeling the emotional sewage Ron was serving up. She grew up with this kind of behavior, but I don't think she had any idea of what she had gotten herself into until a week before I started kindergarten.

◆ ◆ ◆

A few weeks after the parade and ice cream episode I would start kindergarten. Just like any new student going to school for the first time you get to go and meet your teachers and see your classroom for the first time. I remember there was much debate about me during this time. How would it go and how I should behave; the big trips to the department store to buy new clothes and…the haircut. My mother wanted to cut my hair, Ron adamantly protested. In his view, I was a girl and girls had long hair. Mom's view: she had to deal with tangles and getting me ready for school before driving forty-five minutes to get to work on time. Back and forth, on and on and then one day, my hair was cut. My first big haircut was a Dorothy Hamill doo and I was cute.

Right from the haircut we went off to kindergarten orientation where I would meet my teacher, Mrs. Garrison, who was also my mother's teacher when she was in kindergarten. We had to be on time and impressive. After all, Mom's family owned the mill and her grandfather was once the mayor. Everyone knew my mother and her family. That and the fact that the teacher had been around a few years, we owed her the respect of being on time. On our way from my haircut to orientation, we stopped for an ice cream cone. Again, the ice cream! We were driving in our mammoth car and I'm in my favorite white Polly Finders dress with my Dorothy Hamill doo and an ice cream cone. Speeding right along and all of a sudden my ice cream falls off my cone and rolls down the front of my dress. It all went downhill from there. We had to change before the kindergarten interview. We were already running late because we stopped for ice cream. And, when I got home with my new hairdo, more than ice cream hit the fan. For the next three days, I was sent outside to sit on the front stoop while Ron and Mom argued that Mom cut my hair even though Ron said no. They argued and argued and as I said, I spent three days on the front porch. They were both controlling and manipulative so there was no telling who would come out the winner in this one. Eventually it was a draw and on the fourth day I was allowed to stay inside and we never talked about the incident again.

This is what life with Ron and Mom was like. Arguing, passive aggressive behaviors and violent episodes that were never spoken of to anyone, ever. That and I never called Fred anything but my father and every other weekend I would get carted off to my new stepmother, Linda.

During this time life was all about learning to be seen and not heard, to tread lightly on eggshells and slip between the cracks in hopes of disappearing, but I was learning that it wasn't always easy to keep things quiet.

It was a few months after the ice cream and haircut incident that I was on a weekend visit with Fred and Linda. Linda was helping me unpack my suitcase and noticed I had a plastic baseball bat in my suitcase. Linda asked me what it was for and I told her that it was to hit me with if I did not behave. Linda asked my mother about the bat and told her what I said. My mother's response was that I was a manipulative child and I made things up. This was how my mom covered her bases to say I was the manipulator; this went on for my entire childhood.

In addition to being called a manipulator by my mother I began having headaches. I soon had headaches all the time. No reason or explanation just constant headaches. I didn't know life without a headache and I thought they were normal until I was taken to the doctor about them. I eventually went to a neurologist and was given every test they had at that time, and nothing showed up. Just inexplicable headaches.

As I got older, seven to be exact, I was told I had to start doing chores around the house in order to help the family. I would however be given a dollar a week allowance. This was great, a whole dollar, I thought, "You can't beat that!".

So I was now responsible for washing dishes. Each day I got on my stool to reach the sink and I washed dishes. At the end of each week I got my dollar. Oh, I forgot. I also had to set and clear the table before and after dinner. This seemed reasonable since it involved dishes. It wasn't until I started my job that I discovered some hiccups. First, I was required to use unbelievably hot water, or at least I thought it was. Second, I had to get the dishes clean, really clean, no exceptions. I didn't realize how serious this was until one night around 10 pm, I was rudely awakened by Ron. He stormed into my bedroom, turned on all the lights and informed me he found a dirty dish and to come to the kitchen. When I got to the kitchen, he had emptied all the cupboards. Every dish, cup and utensil was in the sink, and on the cupboard, and I was to wash all of them in extremely hot water, right then. Apparently, I had been lacking in my washing duties and he felt it necessary to alert me of this dishwashing skill shortcoming at 10 pm that night. I remember trying to smooth things over, as my mother came into the kitchen to get a glass of water. I smiled nervously and said, "This water is really hot." All I got from her was an eye roll and a smirk of disgust as if to say I should have known better.

◆ ◆ ◆

From the moment they began to date, this emotional roller coaster was their attraction to each other. Emotional outbursts and uncontrollable rage countered by manipulation. Ron lost it and Mom acted like it was no big deal. She covered it all up and manipulated the environment to keep peace while getting exactly what she wanted. I was her pawn and she used me effectively to her advantage.

My job at the age of seven was to smile and tread lightly, across every eggshell. To be a human sensor focused on detecting the mood for each day. Who would I have to be today? Which version of "perfect little girl" would I have to play today and how would I navigate my survival between the two of them?

I became highly skilled in how to survive in any given situation. I was able to know who I had to be, and when to be it. For each person I was required to be a different version of me. Whether it was Ron wanting a perfect little girl, Mom wanting me to help her, Linda wanting me to be invisible, or Fred wanting me to assure I was okay with him, it didn't matter. I was a master at meeting the needs of others and surviving; all before the age of seven.

Chapter Five

Life in The Big City

I remember how my mom hated the winter. Each winter she got depressed and just shut down. I remember we would drive south for a day on the weekend until we saw green, which usually took until we hit Kentucky. It was an adventure getting in our mammoth car with Motown music blaring all the way. The best part was on Monday morning in school for Show and Tell when I got to say I went to Kentucky for the day.

One winter we took a vacation south. Ron and Mom used their tax refund money to pay for the trip and this time we didn't stop until we landed in Naples, Florida. It was fun. We stayed at a place with a pool and a golf course. During the day Mom and I swam and Ron golfed. By the end of the trip Mom even bought a set of clubs and a golf outfit for herself. I remember the pictures and have to laugh because I don't ever remember not liking a picture of my mother until I saw her in a golf outfit. She looked like she came from a special needs home; not her best look. It was similar to when people who go on a cruise to Jamaica or the Bahamas and come back with Bo Derek braids: seemed like the thing to do at the time. This was a really nice time and I remember hearing Ron promise my mother that she would not spend another winter in Michigan. He even brought back a palm branch to stick in the snow so Mom would have something green to look at.

Spring came and then summer and before I knew it fall had arrived, and sure enough Ron held true to his promise. That November, he headed to Florida to find a house and a job and Mom got busy and excited about living in paradise. We packed everything up and sold our house in our super small town where everyone knew our name and moved to the big city down south where no one knew our name.

I remember the preparations for the move, packing and going to court for custody hearings. I was required to talk with a man who I now know was the friend of the court. He asked me questions about moving and what I thought a fair amount of time to spend with Fred would be. That was a tough question because I didn't want to see him or spend time with him ever because when I was with him I never saw him. What they should have asked me is how much time do you want to spend with Linda and the motley crew she called a family? I wanted to blurt out "none, never!" but it was too much pressure. I wanted the bath commercial, "Calgon take me away" to appear with a bubble bath that would wash it all clear and I would never have to visit. Instead, I said what I thought I should say, two to three weeks at first, then, maybe more later. I remember this specifically because by this point in my young life, I had become a master negotiator. My goal was to be liked, keep things calm and keep a low profile. In the end, I was stuck going for a whole month every summer and every other Christmas. Of course, this pissed Ron and Mom off and I heard about it for days as they bore their frustration and anger on me. I was grilled over and over about what I said in my private meeting after they got the shared summer and holiday custody schedule.

Now, as all of this planning and packing for Florida was happening I was sworn to secrecy. By no means was I to tell Fred about any of this. If he knew, it would ruin everything. They never told him. They never shared a drop of information. Then one weekend he came to pick me up and we were gone. By the time Fred got wind of the whole thing, we had been in Florida for nearly two weeks. Details are a little fuzzy but my guess is that because we moved over Thanksgiving he never bothered to check. Or, he was too busy partying to care. What I do remember is that our cousins, who lived next door, called us to let us know he showed up looking for me and to let us know they gave him our new phone number. I also remember Ron and Mom were really pissed. It was like a black cloud hovered over our new house in sunny paradise while Ron sat in his chair and sulked for hours. After two days of this I thought something was really wrong so went to my room to make a list of demands. I wanted to be prepared for when I was forced to talk to Fred. I asked for new clothes, to never go back to Michigan and to never go to Linda's family's house again. I had no idea why they were so angry. I didn't understand that they basically packed up and didn't inform Fred at all. I just felt the disease everywhere and when I showed my mother the list she looked at me like I was stupid, rolled her eyes and handed the list back to me. The moment is still very clear. She just walked away, no hug, no "don't worry" no question about what was on the list, just an eye roll and a disgusted look. This made me feel more confused and because it was about me it made me feel like I was the cause of all of this in the first place.

♦ ♦ ♦

A few weeks later everyone seemed happy and busy adjusting to Florida life. I, however, was trying to adjust to the biggest culture shock of my young life. Nothing prepared me for life in a big city in the South. It was loud and confusing. School was mind-boggling to me. Classes went from 15 students to what seemed like a million. Teachers did not know me; everyone talked funny and looked strange. It was shocking and traumatic to go from a small town and small schoolrooms, to a big city school filled with multi-cultural students and bullying. It was hard and I was not doing well. I was in the fourth grade when we moved and along the way I lost or missed some key lessons and ended up lacking in my math skills. I just couldn't get the multiplication tables memorized. I spent hours listening to records that played them over and over in a song...and nothing. In the classroom I was intimidated and scared. Like I said, it was loud and busy but, that wasn't the whole problem. The teachers didn't have time to really work with me. And on top of that I was the new kid who attracted every bully in the school. I cried at the drop of a hat. If you looked at me wrong, I burst into tears.

One specific event that still lives in my memory is my first time in the lunchroom. I remember sitting across from, as I recall, a very strange, odd-looking girl. She had a big head, long fingers and glaring eyes that peered, right through me. She made me feel naked. As I cautiously watched her with curiosity and apprehension, I noticed she was gnawing on what looked like a pig's foot. Yes, it was a pig's foot, pickled with juice that was all over her face. Shocking at the time and beyond funny now. Later, I got to know this girl and went to high school with her. She was shy and quirky. Once I got to know her, she was still strange but, harmless. I eventually got used to a big city school, riding my bike several miles each day and pickled pig's feet.

But I never got used to the louse.

I got lice so often and so bad, Ron and Mom took me to see a pediatrician. In our family you had to have a limb severed before calling a doctor was even considered, let alone actually making an appointment. I remember the doctor telling my mom and Ron that louse was so rampant in elementary schools you could lean your head against a wall in the building and get them. He said not to worry and was more interested in having a conversation with me than worrying about the pesky parasites that periodically invaded my hair. The lice problem was a traumatic thing for my mom. She just could not deal because she couldn't control the situation. The next time it happened she was over it and made me go into the store by myself to buy the lice shampoo. I was so embarrassed that when I went to the counter to ask the pharmacist for help, I said it was for my brother because I didn't want a soul to know it was for me.

♦ ♦ ♦

Life in Florida was hard for all of us. Although it was green and filled with beautiful palm trees, paradise was rocky. Jobs didn't pay the same and Ron couldn't make the money he made in Michigan doing auto body work. The problem? No snow, no unions, and no booming auto industry in your backyard. In Michigan, it snowed every year and the roads would ice. This required salt on the roads to prevent slips and accidents. But, it also destroyed your car because the salt ate through the metal frame and rusted through the body of your car. This required auto body work to repair and repaint. So thanks to salt, snow, and living an hour away from Detroit, Ron always had work. When we moved away from the auto industry and the winter snow, he still tried to make a living doing the same thing. So it goes without saying they didn't think this out very well. I remember things being very hard during this time. They never had a lot of money and things were not going as planned. Ron cheated on Mom and then she cheated on him, back and forth and back and forth.

With all the unhappiness and financial struggles Ron decided to leave for a while. I neglected to mention he had a habit of leaving. One day he would just say, "I'm leaving" and be gone for two or three months. One time back in Michigan, I remember waking up in the middle of the night and hearing my mother cry on the phone to the doctor she worked for. She told him she wanted to die and was so depressed. She sobbed on the phone for what seemed like hours repeating how everything was so out of control. Ron was gone and she couldn't live

without him.   Ron had left to go to Vegas to win his for-
tune and didn't return until he was broke and emaciated
from not eating because he had no money.

This time was a little different. We were in a new area
meeting new people and having new adventures. This
time my mom went out on dates when he left. I was left
alone. With no one around, I felt lost and scared. It's funny
how when you just want some space and then you get it;
it's scary. I was nine and felt like I was alone, no parents,
no family, no one. As I tried to explain how I was feeling to
my mom, her remedy was to interrupt me and then con-
fide her miseries and secrets to me. She showed me all
her weak spots. Her personal papers, her jewelry, where
she hid it and more. At the time, I didn't understand. It just
felt nice to have her talk to me and treat me like she cared.
She told me not to tell anyone; it was our secret. Then
she left me with a baby sitter and went out partying with
her new friends. As luck would have it, Ron showed up
that evening after being gone again. He was looking for
my mom because she had not returned his phone calls.
When he got to the house he told me about a Halloween
party he wanted to take me to but because Mom was
gone he couldn't. While he was there she called to check
on me. Ron took the phone away from me and they argued. After a while, he became so enraged he started to
smash everything in the house. Throwing pottery, glass
dishes and smashing pictures. He was out of his mind

and I remember asking him if he was going to hit my mom when she got home. His response was "I won't hit her on her body she bruises too easy. I will hit her on the head so no one would notice." Somehow in that moment his logic seemed okay. I guess it was because I was still in shock from having the entire house leveled in less than ten minutes. When Ron calmed down he told me more about the Halloween party he wanted to take me to but couldn't. He explained that he did not have legal custody and if he took me she could have him arrested. At some point he convinced me to tell him where her secret papers and jewelry were hidden. He wanted them so he could use them as leverage to get her to talk to him. I agreed.

In my heart I wanted them to get back together because in my mind he was what held it all together. Mom always felt she needed someone to take care of her and Ron filled that need. The way we lived to please him, reading his moods, treading lightly on eggshells, accepting outbursts and cruel behavior. It all seemed normal and over the years, I even began to feel grateful because I knew people who had it much worse. At least that is what I told myself so I wouldn't feel bad about being used as bait by Ron. Tell the nine-year-old you're taking her to a party; she will tell you where the treasures are hidden. This was how we lived and how they used me. Fight, make up; manipulate the situation: go back to square one and use the kid as bait. Meanwhile, I still had headaches, all the time headaches, and I missed school often. It was getting to the point that I was afraid to be away from home and afraid to be home. So while the headaches were painful they also felt safe because I had a reason to go and be quiet and alone.

Mom and Ron eventually got back together and things started all over. This time Ron was going to be a truck driver and make more money and I was getting ready for my summer trip to see Fred.

Going to my father's was always an interesting, yet complex bag of emotions. It felt heavenly to get on a plane and go away but, when I landed I found myself in the hands of Linda and her motley crew of juvenile delinquents she called brothers and sisters. Each summer was somewhat the same, but this one held an unexpected surprise. We were in the upper part of Michigan around one of the lakes. Not a big one but a lake nonetheless. We had a room for the weekend and Josh, Fred and Linda's son, and I spend most of the day in the water. After dinner Fred, Josh and I went back down to the water to wade and enjoy the evening sunset and the cooling down of the day. Josh was very young. I remember he was still in diapers. Fred was fully engaged in us kids and no one was drunk or looking to get drunk so it was a nice and peaceful moment. As we sat there enjoying the view, Josh went into the water. At first he was just getting his feet wet. Then he went out a little more until the water touched his knees. As I sat there watching him I remember that one moment he was standing and the next he was face down in the water. Beyond that my memory is blurred about the details of this event. One minute he was standing and the next he floated up with a bloated and blue face. The kind of blue face you see when someone stops breathing. Everything happened so fast but the next thing I remember is Fred screaming and panicking. We pulled Josh out of the water and Fred said, "Tracey, do something!" so I rolled him over and starting CPR. After a few breaths, I rolled him over again and he began to cry and cough. I was dazed. I didn't know what was happened, except that in one moment Josh turned blue and stopped breathing, then an ambulance showed up, they were gone and I was alone. I was left in the hotel room by myself and desperately wanted to talk to my mom. I remember dialing the phone every five minutes placing a collect call to get to her and she never answered. I blocked this event from my mind for years and when the memories finally resurfaced, all I could remember was that they left me alone in the hotel room, but that wasn't true. Fred had tried to coerce me into going to the emergency room and I wouldn't go because I was scared and I wanted to talk to my mom. I wanted to stay at the hotel alone because I assumed that I had to be alone to talk to her because when I was in Florida and wanted to talk to Fred I couldn't be myself and had to pretend to be something or someone other than me. So naturally I assumed it would be the same when I was with Fred and Linda.

* * *

Thinking back, it is a mystery to me how I knew to administer CPR. I was only nine, maybe ten years old at the time. I had never heard of CPR or seen it done and yet I performed a version of it on Josh. The only explanation I have been able to come up with over the years is that this was divine guidance and protection walking with me.

* * *

That summer trip to Michigan was hard and I was more than ready to return to my routine of chaos and eggshell-walking in Florida. It was just too much; I had never been as scared as when I saw Josh turn blue. I don't think I was even that scared when Ron destroyed the house. One thing for sure, I never spoke a word of the event and when I got back to Florida no one ever asked me about it. Not once was I asked how it felt to see my baby brother, another human being, almost die. To my mother it simply did not exist, it was the "idiot's life" and I was not allowed to discuss those matters. What happened in Michigan stayed in Michigan.

When I got home that summer life was shifting in what seemed a good direction. Ron was settled into a new career of cleaning offices and homes. He also specialized in cleaning places where people had died. Because the office cleanings were done after hours he was gone every evening. He would leave the house around 6 pm and got home around 1 am. It was great because it made it easy for me to take care of my mom and do what she wanted. I only had one person to please and because of this it felt as though there was peace and calm each evening.

However, the calm did not last. Not long after Ron started this new career, he also started to drink more heavily at night when he got home. He would then sleep a better part of the day before going back to work in the evening. If he had to clean a house where someone had died, or a house where there was a suicide or body just left, he worked 12 to 14 hours a day, until the house was restored and the job finished. The dead bodies didn't seem to bother him or at least that's what he said. When he was in Vietnam, he signed up for grave registration duty and saw a lot of disturbing things so for him this seemed like no big deal. He never went into detail about his horrific experiences and back then you didn't talk about the atrocities of war. For Ron, this was just another piece of trauma and pain.

Even though he said cleaning up after the bodies were left didn't disturb him, he eventually cracked and attempted to overdose on pills. What sent him over the edge was the family dog being killed by the neighbor's Irish Setter. Our little yappy Chihuahua became a chew toy for our neighbor's red beast right before Ron's eyes. Ron freaked. This was his best friend and pal when he came home late at night. As sad as it was, this wasn't the first brush with death our Chihuahua, Jose, had experienced. One winter my mom ran over him with her enormous white Cadillac Seville. The only thing that saved him was his body fat and the mound of snow that softened the impact. His second brush with death was when he had a stroke in our front yard. He survived because my mother gave him mouth-to-mouth resuscitation, but this would be his third and final brush with death. Ron was devastated; Jose was Ron's best friend. That dog meant more to Ron than anyone or anything else. The day it happened Ron stayed up all night and drank himself into a stupor. He then woke me up at two in the morning to tell me how much he loved me and to assure me it would all be okay. I remember being startled and scared seeing him like this. His rage and fits of violence were easier to handle than this, at least I knew what to expect with angry behavior. Thankfully, my mom came in and took him to bed. A few weeks later he did the same thing only this time he told me he loved me and would miss me. This time he added massive amounts of pills to his nightly binge. Again, my mother came to get him. Only this time she was disgusted by his actions and just walked away. When he tried to follow her, he fell and passed out, half in my room and half in the hall. For the rest of the night I heard him vomit and cry. While all of this was happening, my mother was locked safely in her room. The only thing I could do was to try to roll him over so he would not choke on his vomit. The next day Ron was Baker Acted and spent most of the next year in and out of depression programs.

Shortly after the attack by the Irish Setter and Ron's breakdown, I found out about CAP from my math teacher, Mr. Smith. CAP or Civil Air Patrol is an auxiliary of the United States Air Force. I was very excited. For most of my young life I really just kind of worked on keeping peace and reading the vibe of people's moods in an effort to know what was coming. I didn't dream of being a school teacher, super hero or anything else, but I did know I wanted to be a fighter pilot and an astronaut. The thought of flying above everything while keeping a protective watch over all below filled my mind to the point of obsession. I knew for sure this was what I wanted: to escape, while silently providing protection. It was a combination of my passion for leaving it all behind to go above the clouds, the need to protect and the movie "Taps" with Timothy Hutton and George C. Scott that topped off the excitement for my newfound passion. I loved it all: CAP, the uniforms, the marching, the being in charge and giving it all for a worthy cause. I didn't think there could be a better way to live or to die. I really felt I found my place in life, a worthy goal to strive for, flying and playing soldier. I also remember Mr. Smith taking a special interest in me by making sure I got what I needed to help me reach my goal. He took me to my first air show with his family. He made sure my name was on the list of students to be in the first computer class in my school district. He watched over me from the background like a protecting father.

CAP offered me an amazing amount of freedom. I was able to leave the house often and without many questions. I made lots of friends and felt as though I finally fit in and had a purpose. I learned everything I could as fast as I could. I saved all of my money and bought my own uniforms and paid for all the special schools and trainings.

The first training school I went to was a summer encampment on the Naval Base in Orlando. I spent weeks getting ready. Packing, following the required packing list, ironing my uniforms, and going over the packing list again. I was ready and I was excited. Upon arrival, I saw all of my friends who had gone a week earlier to be trained on how to run the program. There were probably two hundred kids and another hundred retired military and volunteer adults there to supervise. I was leaving for a week and I was prepared. It wasn't until we were halfway there that I started to panic. I began to get scared and sick to my stomach. My pulse raced and I was having trouble breathing. I realized that I would be leaving my home for a whole week and anything could happen. There was no one to look after my mom and I was supposed to take care of things for her. It was a tough week for me and I never stopped worrying about everything. Would she be safe? Would Ron destroy the house? Somehow I worked through the panic attacks and migraine headaches but they never went away completely. Fortunately, I wanted to fly more than I wanted my fear. I was focused and passionate about stepping into the vision I had for myself and the drive to continue became greater than the fear, panic or pain. How did I get through? I learned to negotiate with myself. I did only what was required as far as being away for long periods of time and if I wasn't gun ho about attending an event I did not go.

Life was a bit easier now because I had CAP to keep me busy. I still carried anxiety and fear when I was away from home and always felt the "What if something happened?" cloud that followed me. There were still a lot of headaches; about three or four a week and by now they had progressed to full blown migraines. I remember the first really brutal migraine I had hit me the summer before I started high school while in a movie theatre with Ron and Mom. As I sat there watching the movie I started seeing lots of bright lights and movement and before long I couldn't see the movie at all. It felt like I had just stared into a light and then looked away. I immediately felt nauseous and ran out of the theatre barely making it to the bathroom as I left pieces of my lunch in the lobby. I was sick, felt miserable and needed to go home. I remember this event caused a big problem because Mom and Ron did not get to see the end of the movie. They grumbled all the way home and when we got there they dropped me off and hurried back to the theatre.

At the end of summer, I started high school and joined Junior Reserves Officers Training Corp (JROTC). Joining JROTC was just one more step on my career path to becoming a pilot and soaring above the clouds. When I started high school and JROTC and had already become an accomplished officer in CAP. I was a lieutenant and had been to encampments and drill team competitions all over the state. I was a real hard ass and was affectionately known as the "Ice Maiden".

Even with all of my accomplishments and adventures that most would only dream of, I still struggled with life. I don't ever remember being happy. I always felt like a geek, out of place or just misunderstood. Things at home were always in a state of disease, and I never knew what I was going to get. It was "like a box of chocolates" as Forrest Gump would say. Around this time, I met Orlando, a fellow CAP geek. He and his buddy Rob wanted to take me and a friend out to dinner. Orlando had money and a sports car and I wanted nothing to do with him. Instead, I liked Rob, an even bigger geek. It wasn't until the second date when Orlando took both of us girls out that I realized I wanted Orlando the geek and not Rob the geek. Orlando and I dated for three and a half years. His family was odd. They were awful to each other but they were good to me. Dating Orlando allowed me certain experiences I would have never had. One year a trip to New York City for spring break via train ride with private rooms. We stayed at the Algonquin Hotel and saw Broadway plays. Afterwards, we had cheesecake and coffee in the same room where the writers of the round table met years before.

One of my favorite memories of Orlando is about a bug. Years after Ron's Chihuahua became a snack for the neighbor's Irish setter, we adopted two little long hair Chihuahuas. They were cute and adorable and looked like little rugs walking around the house. Ron let the dogs play with beetles because they were fascinated with any-thing that moved. I remember it like it was yesterday be-cause it made my stomach flip to see someone stand up to Ron whom I had feared since the age of three. As we sat in the family room of our home Ron set up the game of beetle and dog, Orlando began to turn green. He was uncomfortable and began rubbing the back of his neck. Midway through Ron's little show, Orlando got up grabbed the beetle and released it outside. I was mortified. I didn't know what was going to happen next. Orlando came back, smiled and said, "I just can't take that." He could not handle watching the bug get tortured. To my surprise, Ron said nothing. I remember that story because it always reminded me of how compassionate and decent Orlando could be.

Eventually I broke up with Orlando and he started dating my best friend. My reason for breaking up with him was that we were going nowhere. There was no growth in our friendship or relationship. He was really good at giving material things and I did enjoy the material things but I wanted to connect with someone and not feel obligated. I think it must have been hard for him living with all that money and no love. He didn't know any other way so he just did what the rest of the family did; negotiate with money for what he thought would complete him. It's my opinion that this left him unable to connect in any real way. While it was sad and difficult for him I have always remembered his family as being very quirky, kind and generous.

Chapter Six

Some Things Never Change

Time went on and over the years Ron became progressively worse. He got meaner and less active. This made things easier for me because he didn't notice me. One summer his kids from another marriage came to visit us. We had never met them or even heard of them and one summer they just appeared and I had to share my room and my things with them. His daughter, Julia, was two years younger than me and his son, Zack, was three years younger. I wasn't aware that Ron had any kind of contact with them. But, obviously, he did.

It was awful. For starters, Julia was a thief and a liar and Zack had serious emotional issues. The whole time they were in our home my mother manipulated the scene. She told me how I should act and what I should say to keep the peace and also showed Ron how awful his kids were. This was my mom's attempt to push him away from his kids and keep things as she wanted them. It was hell and by the end of the summer I was sleeping on the living room couch. Julia had swiped nearly all of my belongings including my underwear. I felt invaded and had no coping skills for this kind of disruption. At the time it was more than I could bear. It was a summer filled with migraines and total turmoil. That was an impossible summer for us and it had to be for them. I can't imagine how hard it had to be for them. Visiting a father they did not know, while dealing with a conniving and manipulative stepmother whose sole purpose was to get rid of them.

At the end of the summer Julia and Zack went home and six months later, Zack returned to live with us. Zack was constantly in trouble. His mother had become so frustrated with him that she gave up and sent him to live with his father Ron permanently. Now this didn't make me happy. Life was already difficult enough but my mother? She was out of her mind. She could barely manage her husband, and now there was a mirror image of him in our home. It was a dark time and I remember that when Ron was at work my mother would allow me, no, let me rephrase that, encouraged and insisted I be abusive and cruel to Zack. She would pull one of her: *I can't deal. Please help me with Zack, he won't do this or that. Go make him.* And I did. I'm not proud of this but it happened. His life was hell.

About a year into Zack living with us my mother manipulated and twisted the situation so much that it was nearly impossible for Zack or Ron to cope. The more she twisted, pushed and fabricated the more he acted out. The more he acted out the harder life got for both Ron and Zack. Ultimately, Ron sent Zack back to live with his mother who didn't want him in the first place. After my mother got rid of Zack, things went back to the simpler and more familiar eggshell walking.

(Considering this experience, I feel it important to note that years later, Zack showed up at our front door to let us know he was back in Florida. I remember my mom saying, "Don't let him in the house he lives on the street and is a thief." Eventually, Zack made amends with his father. He even reconnected with my mother and started a new relationship with her. My mother eventually made peace with him and set me up to see him. Surprisingly, he was more than open to forgive. I remember saying, "I can't believe you would speak to us after all the horrible shit we did to you." His response, "It's all forgotten." It takes a big person to say something like that and mean it. But, he did.)

Soon after Zack went back to his mother's, my mom started tapping into her creative side by making crafts and art with seashells. She began taking a variety of craft classes about shell crafting, beading, sewing, drawing and even painting by numbers. She was crafting all the time and decided to start a club. She signed up for a how-to class with an extremely talented and successful crafter in Panama City, Florida. She and two other friends went off to play and craft with seashells and what not, and I was left home with Ron. During her week long absence, he gave me the keys and permission to drive her sports car to school and do pretty much anything I pleased. It was really nice and surprisingly calm. I even broke my three-school-day week schedule by showing up five days in a row that week. I showed up every day that week and no headaches. It was the first time I ever noticed how calm and relaxing it could be without her around. It was a great way to wrap up my sophomore year.

At one point during my mom's crafting excursion she called home and asked me to run an errand. When I heard her voice on the phone I began to cry. I don't know why, I just cried. I remember she became alarmed and asked me for the first time ever if Ron had hurt me. This seemed odd to me because on some level he hurt me every day, and, if the hurt wasn't coming from him it came from her. So why was I crying? I was crying because as much as I enjoyed the calm without her, I still missed her and was worried about her. Worried about her being safe, worried that I was not able to take care of her when she was so far away, and then worried because I really didn't know how to act in the face of peace and calm. Her phone call was interesting to me because she knew what Ron was like and still she left me with him. After Mom came home she became busy crafting and making new friends.

As Mom took classes locally, I was getting ready for my junior year in high school. I was becoming more and more independent. I had a car and could drive myself to school and to CAP activities. I even drove to Gainesville to visit my friends at the University of Florida. Every chance I got I was gone. I was enjoying my independence and was climbing the ladder in JROTC and CAP. I was on fire.... until I got home in the evenings.

I remember one evening I had a friend over for dinner. We were all sitting around the table and Ron was acting weirder than his normal weird. He was being mildly abusive and over all rude. At one point, I asked him if he had taken his meds because he was acting odd and then the next thing we knew he was going off. He started screaming and yelling and then he hit me. My friend freaked and called her parents to pick her up. She was out of there and who could blame her? I guess my comment wasn't the most conducive to a calm reaction from Ron, yet I was having a brave moment and couldn't resist. It was embarrassing to have someone see what my life was really like, but I never realized that other people did not live like this until she told me she had never even seen her parents argue. Maybe that was why I choose that moment to be brave and say something that would trigger him. Maybe I needed to understand that this kind of behavior was not normal.

I was now seventeen and Ron and Mom had been creating this kind of chaos in our lives for fourteen years. I was tired, had migraine headaches, was sad most times and had thought of ending my life on a regular basis. I remember telling my mom how I was feeling and she said to me, "This is the way life is. You get six good months and six bad months if you're lucky." This did not make me feel better nor did it give me hope.

Shortly after this conversation with my mom was the JROTC military ball. Our Colonel was excellent at getting our unit funding and setting up really great events for us. We had a true military ball with a receiving line, a formal sit down dinner and dance. Every year I went with Orlando but not this year. I had broken up with him and needed a date. So that year I decided I was taking a new guy and I asked the school's foreign exchange student from Germany. I can't even remember his name but he was way cool and cute. I got home and shared my news and Ron who said, "You can't go with him." I responded, "I already asked." Ron retorted, "It doesn't matter, you're not allowed to go to the dance with a boy." I was devastated. I did not know how to tell this guy I couldn't go with him. I felt like no matter what I did, it was wrong. One minute

Ron would lay down the rule that I had to wear dresses to school and the next I couldn't go to a dance with a boy. Who did he want me to take? Surely not a girl, that would be wrong too. As I laid on my bed in tears feeling confused and distraught, my mother came in and said, "Don't worry about it, you're going."

Weeks later, Ron checked himself into the Veterans Administration hospital (VA) and told me he and my mother would have a platonic relationship. He said he loved me very much and would continue to have a relationship with me; I was his daughter no matter what. That was the last conversation I had with him for almost a year. My mother's version of the break-up went more like it was her decision. She decided that if Ron couldn't at least be nice to me, then there was no reason to continue their relationship. Ron moved out of the house and he and my mother divorced.

Chapter Seven

When Things Change Big They Also Change Fast

With Ron gone things got even more interesting. There was a calm and sense of freedom in the house followed by an underlying fear and disturbing panic. I felt it everywhere. Mom was constantly worried about paying bills and who would take care of her. I was relieved. It was the end of my junior in high school and summer was on its way. I was planning my future and having a blast with my newly found freedom.

It was the night of the big event, the yearly military ball and my foreign exchange student date. On top of all that, this year was the year I would be announced as battalion commander. I had worked hard. I commanded the first place girl's drill team for the state two years running. I was the first place individual driller in the state two years running. I had been in CAP since the seventh grade and was the highest-ranking female in the state. Not to mention I was awarded a student ambassador position to Europe that summer and was scheduled to attended glider pilot school where I would earn my solo wings. I was now seventeen. I had worked hard. I had arrived. As the night progressed, the tension grew. The only person who could possibly beat me for this position was Zoe, my longtime friend/enemy. Zoe was never really my enemy. In fact, she became one of my best friends. But for now she was the competition and my enemy. This was serious stuff. I had a lifetime invested in this and I always achieved my goal. Finally, the moment came and the announcement was made. I was named the Battalion's Executive Officer and Zoe the Battalion Commander. I was devastated; it was as though the rug was pulled out from under my whole world. I had a plan and this was a serious monkey wrench. I even have pictures of me crying in public with my arm around Zoe because someone thought it would be a good idea to get a picture of the two new leaders. I had spent seven years, in some sort of military organization, volunteering my time and building the foundation for my future. I was good at what I did. I had a way with people. Even though I was the "Ice Maiden" I was fair and I was dedicated. In the end, it all boiled down to attendance. Zoe showed up every day for school and I did not. I chose to create my own schedule and she followed the standard five days a week schedule. This was a tough lesson for me. Understanding the importance of accountability and participation took years for me to grasp.

Later that evening my guidance counselor came over to me, gave me a hug and whispered in my ear, "Don't worry. You blew her away on your ACT scores." It was one of those moments like in the movie "The Christmas Story". Ralphie is lying in bed feeling defeated about his quest to acquire a red rider BB gun, and all of a sudden he remembered...Santa!! So I had an early visit that year from Santa. Somehow that little moment made every-thing just melt away and all was well. I remember the rest of the evening as being fun and light, almost a relief. As I let go of being number one in charge and I started to get excited about what the adventures of summer would hold for me as I was going to fly gliders and travel to Europe as an ambassador for the United States with CAP.

After that evening it felt as though my whole life shift-ed in a blink of an eye. I was no longer living in fear of Ron, worrying about being battalion commander or about my mom. I was off to school to learn how to soar. I was step-ping into a chance to have fun before my senior year.

Off to Missouri for a week, I was the only girl in my class and one of eight in the nation to be awarded at-tendance at this flight school. I was nervous...okay, I was more than nervous. I was scared. I was going to be alone in that glider. If something went wrong that was it. No second chances on this one, this is where things get real. I think it's funny because the summer before, I did water survival training off the coast of Miami with the F-16 pilots. I parasailed out, I was released and then drifted into the water. I had to be sure to release my parachute so I didn't drown or get dragged for miles. I was then left to float in the Gulf for hours in a raft with holes. That was the survival part, staying safe in a raft with holes. Granted, we were checked on but that was serious stuff. At the end of the day we got picked up by a helicopter to which you couldn't connect too soon or you would get the jolt of a lifetime. I went through all of this and it was more detailed than glider flying and still I was terrified of the glider and during the training, I was focused. It was the first time I ever attended an event and didn't call home. Not once.

By the end of the school I soloed, I was a glider pilot. I had earned my wings. I also got something else. I got a call from my mom. She actually called to check on me because she missed me. It was the first time ever that she called me while I was away. This was nice and confusing. She never called for that reason or to say she missed me. Not even when I went to visit Fred. But with Ron gone she had a lot of extra time on her hands and no one to talk to.

Later in the summer, I headed for Austria to participate as the student ambassador with the U.S. government and CAP. While in Austria we were sponsored by all the Austrian glider clubs. This meant I would get to fly gliders all summer in the Alps, take trains through the beautiful Austrian countryside, ride on the Autobahn and go through cold war checkpoints. I had lunch on the highest point in Innsbruck, Austria, drinking coffee and liking it for the first time in my life while eating traditional apple strudel. I stayed at the Olympic center for athletes in Gras and attending a garden party next to the glider airstrip. Step out of your glider and step into a party. The trip was topped with tickets to the Salzburg Festival, the national opera that even most native Europeans rarely get to see. I was on top of the world and experiencing the goals I set back in middle school. I achieved everything I set out to do. It was the best feeling I had ever experienced in my entire eighteen years of life. Jet setting around Europe and falling for an amazing guy from Switzerland, a gorgeous blonde named Sven. Sven was part of the Swiss version of CAP and he was funny and beautiful. I had never had such a cute guy like me. Normally, my "Ice Maiden" approach worked to keep everyone away but, not this time and not with this guy.

After returning home from my summer of adventures, I started to prepare for my senior year in high school with school pictures, class rings, yearbook and new school clothes. Only we had no money for any of these things. For the first time in my life I started school with no new clothes. I wasn't too happy about it. In fact, I was devastated and felt almost embarrassed about it. Everyone would know and they would make fun of me for sure.

Funny because I had just spent the best summer of my life and yet I was in tears about new clothes. I didn't see the bigger picture because I only knew how to get through another six months of what seemed like nothing special compared to traveling around the world and flying above it all. I was depressed and riddled with headaches. I missed my European glider friends and my beautiful Swedish Sven. I was distraught much of the time and slept most of my days away. I also gained some weight but didn't notice this until my mother pointed it out to me.

All of that and this school year a new attendance law was implemented. If you missed more than ten days in a semester you automatically failed. This seriously messed up my routine of three days on, two days off. I was forced to attend school like everyone.

Midway through the school year I didn't think I was going to make it. I had thoughts of dropping out of school and consistently wished I would die. My mother handled the situation by drugging me with diet pills to get me through. Since she had pointed out I gained weight I guess she thought she was helping me with two things at once: weight gain and depression. When I tried to talk to her about what was going on or to just feel close, she usually made fun of me by saying how sick and tired she was of hearing about how I felt. She was too busy dating and worrying about how to pay the bills. Instead of taking the time to talk with me she gave me her philosophy on life and more diet pills. Remember, "You get six good months and six bad months and that's all you should expect. Just deal with it."

Shortly after this little reminder of life according to Mom, I got a letter from Sven telling me he was coming to America to visit. This was the best news I had gotten in a long time. I was so excited, it was just what I needed, something special to look forward to. I got permission to take him to school with me as an observer. This was a big break for me because I didn't have any sick days left and I was not repeating my senior year. It was around this time I found out I was accepted into college and because we had no money I was eligible for lots of scholarships. Things were looking good. When Sven showed up, I took him everywhere. I introduced him to all my friends and one friend in particular, Greg. My friend Greg was a jazz musician who loved being in JROTC. He was amazing. Not only was he one of the best cadets we had, he was a cool, fun and all around goofy friend who felt like a breath of fresh air whenever he was around.

In addition to being a great friend, Greg was also one of the most gifted musicians in school. Our senior year, he won the Clearwater Jazz Festival. He was also the Student Class President, the All County Goalkeeper in soccer and he earned a scholarship to Berkley College of

Music in Boston. We had much in common. We both had an overwhelming desire to achieve and to please those around us. Our main difference, he was nice about it and I wasn't always so nice about it.

I thought Sven and Greg would hit it off great. Was I wrong! For starters, Sven was a racist and referred to Greg as an unmentionable and little did I know that Greg had a crush on me and was not happy to meet Sven nor was he happy that I was so excited to see him. I had no idea Greg liked me and I had no idea Sven was a racist. Normally I would ignore the racist thing because while it wasn't who I was, it was everywhere and it was a bigger battle than I knew how to fight. I lived in the south and as child it was common to hear and see racism at work. Even in church it was common to hear the preacher use the "N" word in his sermon. I never liked it and never got used to it so when Sven started his racist comments I wasn't happy with him at all. In fact, it really pissed me off. Why? Because, Greg is black and as much as he liked me I liked him. I had been hanging around Greg a few months before Sven showed up. At least, I thought I had been hanging around him. Later, I found out he was making friends with my friends in an effort to hang out with me. Turns out that the music room and the JROTC classes were next to each other and he watched me practice each day. It was my hourglass figure that got his attention.

My idea that Greg and Sven would get along really backfired and to top it all off on one of the days all three of us were together we were talking about prom. Greg then asked me if I had a date and I said I did not. He then asked me to go to prom right in front of Sven. You could have heard a pin drop as I said yes.

At the end of a really long week I took Sven back to the airport and never heard from him again. As I left the airport I thought about how awful Sven was and how hurt I was that someone could be so cruel to another all because of what they looked like.

Once Sven was gone I started hanging out with Greg more. Each day for lunch we would meet in the music room and he would teach me to play heart and soul on the piano. We would laugh and have fun as we got to know each other better and for the first time in twelve years I was eager to go to school.

Finally, it was the big night. I was going to prom with Greg, the class president, Berkley College of Music Scholarship winner, Clearwater Jazz Festival winner, and everybody's favorite guy. I, Ice Maiden, was going to the prom with Greg. I never felt so amazing. I loved that he was creative. I loved that he had been making friends with my friends to meet me. And I loved that he was funny and kind. I also loved that we looked hot together. I mean we were a gorgeous couple. I remember when we were waiting to be seated for dinner before the dance, we had people coming up to us and saying how nice we looked. We even had one older lady come up to us and say, "Motown is not dead". We gave out great vibes when we were in public. We looked and felt good and others felt it when they saw us. My mom loved Greg and he made me happy. For the first time in my life, I felt loved and appreciated for me. Not what I could do or should do, but just for me. It was nice.

While most of the evening's events are a blur, a few things are still crystal clear. First, Orlando, my first boyfriend and my used-to-be best friend was there and created some drama. Someone had slashed Orlando's car tires and because Greg and I were late getting to the dance, I was accused of the slashing. The second thing I remember is one of Greg's friends wanting to be sure I liked Greg. Liked him not just as a buddy, but as a boyfriend. I told her yes and yes and then yes again. Later that evening we headed to the beach where we kissed for the first time, then at my front door for a second time. The first and second kiss was just a kiss. No sparks or tingly feelings; just lots of lips and smooching. I just figured it was my inexperience and our collective nervousness that made it just nice and not *fireworks* nice!!!

For the rest of the school year, we were connected at the hip. We went everywhere together and had a great time doing it. I actually started to have fun at school and then as the year wound down it was time for my final military ball. This year was very different. I had a beautiful boyfriend and my home situation was very different.

It was no secret my parents were divorced since Colonel Jackson, my JROTC commander since ninth grade, had taken an interest in me and watched over me like a parent would. From the very beginning of high school he adopted Zoe and me. At the time, it felt like meddling, now I know he had nothing but genuine concern for us. The same was true for our sergeant majors. They all took good care of us and made sure we had what we needed. Speaking of which, Colonel Jackson was single and so was my mom. She somehow wormed her way and ended up being his date to my military ball.

♦ ♦ ♦

I never understood her need to be involved with my friends and activities. It was as though she started to lose her mind and forgot she was the mom. Or maybe I was just seeing that she was never the mom. Right before the military ball Ron invited us to visit him in the Florida Keys for spring break. So, we drove down and met him there. It was like she was on her honeymoon. She was so happy and she completely ignored the fact that Ron had re-married a woman he met while Baker Acted. So one moment we were in the Keys with her re-married ex and the next week she was my Colonel's date for my military ball. It was an interesting way to end my senior year.

I was finally graduating and thanks to Fred, I had graduation pictures and invitations to send out. We even had a big party at the house. All of my friends and my mom's friends were there. My CAP friend Constance came down from New York, and Greg brought his family. It was a great party; we all got drunk and acted stupid like kids do. But, we were responsible. We always had a key master, someone who did not drink and took everyone's car keys. The key master made sure no one drove drunk. I guess in my mind that made it okay to be underage and drinking. It also gave the appearance of responsibility to my mother. I even remember my mother bragging to her friends about how responsible we were. Like it was acceptable to let your underage kids drink.

Once the graduation dust settled Greg and I spent every moment together. It wasn't until mid-summer that I told Fred about Greg being black. I know I make it sound like Greg had a disease that needed to be hidden, but back then it was a big deal to be in a bi-racial relationship. I started off by telling Fred all of the positive stuff about Greg. Really building it up so he seemed like a super hero. Then, I dropped the bomb. Silence. The next thing I heard was "I can't believe your mother would allow that shit." I told him he would have to accept Greg or not accept me. We did not speak for a year. Fred wasn't the only one who was upset about me dating a black guy. When Ron found out, he was just nasty and nasty with the purpose of being vile and cruel.

The summer after graduation was filled with lots of big shifts. It all started with ending communication and contact with Ron, telling Fred he would have to accept Greg or not have a relationship with me, and finally Greg and I attending "The Forum." It was a seminar that helped you learn about yourself by getting you to be accountable for your life. No excuses. Just you and what you had created up until that point in your life. Fresh out of high school we both signed up for this overpriced, $600.00 to be exact, class. In 1989 this was a lot of money and it might as well have been $1,000.00. I spent all of my graduation money on the seminar and Greg borrowed money from his aunt. This seminar was going to be the answer for me. Why was I still so sad? Why did I have headaches? Why was it so scary to be away from home? Why was I so angry, clingy and just yucky all the time? I knew the information in this seminar would hold the key to unlocking my questions about my life and allow me to find happiness.

It was a two weekend seminar and part of the commitment of being in the seminar was you had to agree to keep all the information confidential. No sharing what you heard from others or about others. You had to agree to abstain from drugs, drinking and any other addictive behaviors. I was ready. I was committed. I wanted answers.

Midway through the first weekend I stood up with tears in my eyes, blubbering, barely able to speak, "I'm so upset there is nothing for me here and I can't believe I'm getting nothing from this." The seminar leader looked at me, laughed then said, "Nothing's going on?" as I stood there crying. He then went on to say that I had a huge accountability issue and was obviously struggling with my sexuality. I asked no more questions.

At the end of the final weekend, I left with no coping tools or insight but gained more strategies on how to manipulate my own personal denial. Greg left knowing he wanted to be an F-16 pilot, not a musician like his parents had dreamed.

It was after this seminar that I decided to have sex with Greg. I remember asking my mom about it, as though I was asking her permission to use my own body. After our conversation, I went to the public health department, had my first appointment with a gynecologist and got a birth control prescription. The first time with Greg was, well, not what I had hoped it would be. I couldn't get into kissing him so much and it took me a while to enjoy just making out. So the first time in bed was not great. After the first time though, I started to get my rhythm and by the end of the summer we had found our groove.

By summer's end, Greg and I were off to school. Neither one of us wanted to go to school, we were both headed in directions that no longer suited us. But, if I was going to be a pilot and soar above the clouds, I had to start over in the real Reserves Officers Training Corps (ROTC). If Greg was going to be the musician of his parents' dreams, he had to go to Berkley.

My first day in ROTC in college was spent standing in a parking lot getting ready for formation like I had done so many times before. As I stood there I thought, 'I'm nobody' I look just like everyone else, all of these people have been in CAP and JROTC. They had all been to state competitions, flown planes, traveled and were just alike. I'm not starting over again and just like that I was dizzy and ready to pass out. The flight commander said to me, "Don't lock your knees." I remember thinking I know not to lock my knees, this is not my first rodeo. I'm a drillmaster. And in the next thought I'm thinking maybe I could be an art major? Wouldn't that be interesting? The next day I went to the admin office at my school and changed my major.

I wasn't the only one experiencing the heaviness of what starting over felt like. Greg was also feeling it and after three months he was done with Berkley and came home. He quit music school and started ROTC in the winter semester. It was interesting to see him go from musician to soldier as I was going from soldier to artist. He loved the idea of being a soldier more than anything else and I loved the idea of being free from following orders.

♦ ♦ ♦

Greg and I weren't the only ones going through changes. Mom was doing her craft club full time. At the craft seminar she attended in Panama City, the famous crafter helped her see her true love of creating and organizing. So she started teaching people how to build their own organizations full time.

If Mom wasn't building a new group she was partying with friends or off with some guy. One time she took off with a guy she had just met to go to the Florida Keys for a weekend. She didn't care. She would go out to party and bring strange men home or tell me I couldn't come home for a weekend because she had someone coming over. One time she did this and I spent the weekend in my car because I didn't have the money for a hotel room.

♦ ♦ ♦

By my sophomore year in college I was an art major. Since I no longer wished to soar in the clouds in a plane I decided I would show the world how to soar without a plane or jet, but rather with imagination by creating something out of nothing. I really liked art and enjoyed the creative process even more than marching. Getting dirty and making something out of a piece of perceived nothing appealed to me. I spent hours in junkyards pulling scrap metal and other objects I envisioned could be great works of art. If I wasn't in a junkyard, I had my camera snapping photos of anything that piqued my interest. Manhole covers, car tires, trees, you name it. I loved taking pictures so much that I went out West to study with photographers who worked under Ansel Adams. Black and white was my passion and I was forever trying to understand how to get a perfect shot using the zone system.

To pay for school, I learned about student and parent loans. There was money available to students to pay for school. Even though I was figuring out my life and starting to have fun doing it, Mom was still struggling and needed help. She had not paid her property taxes in three or four years and they were going to put a lien on her house as a result. I told her about the student loans that could be used for living expenses and since I still lived at home I said if she took out the loan to help me with school we could use some of the money to pay the back property tax she owed. She agreed. We paid off the property tax and I got the down payment for a decent car to drive back and forth to school every day.

Chapter Eight

Still More Change

One of the good things about being in college was going to the school nurse if I was not feeling well. Since I had a history of not feeling well it was nice to get something done about it. At this time, I had persistent headaches, over-all body aches and pains, and now I was having hearing problems that were becoming more and more of an issue. After a couple of trips to the school nurse I was sent to a specialist for this hearing loss. On my first appointment, the ENT determined that I had calcium deposits built up in my ears. I was given a prescription for something called Florical, a combination of fluoride and calcium, to break the deposits loose. This went on for a year before the ENT ordered an MRI or any other test.

As my sophomore year wound down I decided that going back to college was not for me and Greg was feeling the same way. So neither one of us planned on going back to school the upcoming fall. Instead I took over some of the small cleaning accounts my mom still had from when she and Ron cleaned. Greg started a new business venture selling perfume. As I was figuring out what I was going to do with my life, Greg was learning about what life with criminals was like. It turned out that the fragrance business was a big scam and they took Greg for everything. It literally got to the point where he would have had to live in his car had it not been for his Aunt Rose. Greg's Aunt Rose was a beautiful soul who couldn't stand the thought of her nephew living in his car.

While Greg and I were exploring and experimenting with our life's possibilities, my mom started dating this cool guy, Arthur, who was a world-renowned hairdresser. Arthur did Couture shows in Milan, Paris, and all over the world. He was creative, theatrical and loved to cook. When he came over we spent hours in the kitchen cooking the most exotic dishes; things he discovered on his many adventures. He was fun and genuinely interested in being a nice guy and a friend. He felt like a dad during the time Fred and I were not speaking. In truth, he was more of a dad to me than anyone else had been in my life to that point. I remember this used to really piss my mother off because he was more interested in cooking and visiting with Greg and me than he was in having sex with her. She would use all sorts of excuses as to why we couldn't cook when he came over so she could have him to herself. Eventually he stopped coming around.

After spending time with Arthur I decided I wanted to pursue the culinary arts. I applied to Disney World's culinary program. I went through the extensive interview process and was finally given a position in one of their restaurants to get my practical experience requirements for their school. In order to make all this work I planned to rent a room in Orlando while Greg stayed in St Pete in a cute apartment we just had found. Since Greg had just lost everything in the perfume scam he would take over my cleaning accounts that would just pay the rent. It seemed that everything was going to work out. It was just going to take a little bit of regrouping.

During the interview process for my new job, I was still going through tests and waiting for MRI results. I was getting weaker and slower. Everything felt like a chore and I was tired and had headaches all of the time.

It was the beginning of June and I was moving to Orlando for my new job in July. Things were difficult between Greg and I; we were barely getting along and had no money. Our saving grace was an amazing new landlord. He made it fun to live in his building and helped us out by providing odd jobs to cover the rent. When I first met him I filled out the application and returned it by myself. A few weeks after we moved in he told me he wasn't sure what to expect when he first met Greg since I picked up and delivered the applications. I explained to him that looking for an apartment was a challenge. On several occasions landlords told us there was no vacancy even on a Sunday morning only hours after the paper had been printed. At that time, no one wanted to rent to a bi-racial couple. He just shook his head in disbelief. From that moment on he treated us like his kids. He was like a watchful uncle.

We settled into the apartment and I prepared to start my commute to Orlando each week. I also had an appointment with a neurologist who had viewed my MRI and wanted to run a series of tests. He ran all sorts of annoying and exhausting ones. He even gave me a type of electro shock stimulation. It was terrible and I felt like a certified lab rat after he was done. When we finally got the diagnosis I was referred to another specialist and a week later I was in the hospital having brain surgery. In that moment I had to decide between the new job or brain surgery. I really wanted the new job and asked if I could put this off until my new insurance kicked in. I was told it was not advisable that this matter had to be handled immediately. In that moment I did not really understand what an astrocytoma was.

I freaked out and so did my mother. I remember she actually went to the appointment with me to get the diagnosis. It was the first time I thought this might be serious because she just didn't do that type of thing. She never went to a doctor's appointment with me. I also remember that during the next two days we called family to let them know my diagnosis. Mom even called Fred. Interesting how it took me getting sick for us to speak again, but I remember him wanting to come down for the surgery and I remember telling him not to come down because it was not a big deal. I even called Linda, his wife, and asked her to tell him not to come. She agreed with me but said he insisted on coming.

I was diagnosed with an astrocytoma on the left pond. In English, a brain tumor on the left-brain stem. I had no idea how serious this was at the time and quite honestly I did not want to know. I went through all the procedures and protocol and to be honest, it was a relief. I did not have to worry about anyone else except me. Ever since I could remember when I was tired or overwhelmed, which felt like every day, I would ask for something really "good" to happen to me. Something that would let me have a break, a reason for someone else to take care of me. When I wished for "good" I didn't mean happy good. I meant seriously good enough for "things to be over". I wanted an end to the way my life was. The walking on eggshells. The taking care of my mom. The always being on guard. I wanted life as I knew it to be over.

While I was in the hospital my mom and Greg had me on a twenty-four-hour regimen of fresh carrot juice. They juiced and delivered quarts of carrot apple juice to me twice a day for the entire time I was in the hospital. I drank so much carrot juice the palms of my hands turned orange. The reasoning behind the carrot juice was the beta-carotene. Carrots are a rich source of beta-carotene, and when you juice them you get more of the nutrients. The fresh juice more easily assimilates into the cells of the body, and since beta-carotene is a known cancer fighter my mom thought we could juice the tumor away.

I was completely unaware of the gravity of the situation until my first meeting with my oncologist in the hospital. He was the first person to use the word cancer in describing my situation. I remember meeting him and hearing what he had to say and then feeling like a thick fog had just covered me. His first visit was a day after surgery and he explained that nothing would be left on the table. They would do everything in their power to shrink the tumor and be sure I survived. He then explained the regimens of radiation and experimental forms of chemotherapy they would use to fight the cancer. He explained I would be given the maximum amount of radiation you can have in a lifetime. It was very clear that this was a one shot deal. It was also the first time I was really scared and it was the first time I actually heard the word cancer.

When the surgery was over and the doctors were done using me as a guinea pig I had gained over eighty pounds in a month. I was given massive amounts of steroids in an effort to minimize the brain swelling from surgery. While in the hospital I received two spinal taps, also to reduce brain swelling. There were two because the doctor missed the first time and hit a nerve. In the next two years, I received more MRIs than I have fingers and toes and went through severe bouts of depression. The level of chemical imbalance that resulted from the procedures was worse than anything I had ever experienced. It changed everything on every level, my mind and body were never the same again, it's indescribable.

◆ ◆ ◆

I was finally done with my treatments and three months later went back for my ninety-day PET scan. I was nervous. It was the longest and hardest thirty-five minutes of my life. Waiting in the doctor's office was brutal and I couldn't understand why it was taking so long. I was pacing back and forth and finally we got the word. The scan was so positive they insisted on revising the report to reflect a less positive result. The tumor had shrunk so significantly they were stunned. All of the prayers, blessings and carrot juice had worked. My prognosis looked better than they had hoped.

It's interesting to note that at the time I was diagnosed, you did not hear about or see a lot of twenty-one-year-olds getting astrocytoma. In fact, only babies and older people got them. It was such a rare occurrence that the medical diagnosis was written up in medical journals and cited for peer review papers. So when I asked for something good I got the best. I also got the best doctors in their field to work with me. The doctors who performed the surgery and administered the radiation and chemo treatments were tops in their field. I definitely got everyone's attention.

One thing I would like to say about this experience is that while having a brain tumor was a horrible thing to have happen, it also gave me some amazing blessings. For starters, I was now talking to Fred for the first time in nearly three years and he met Greg and loved him. In the years that followed Fred came down every winter for a visit. He also made it a point to have dinner with me on my birthday. Rebuilding this relationship with my real dad was a beautiful and continued blessing I received from a not-so-beautiful event.

Another beautiful blessing that came from the experience was Greg. He stuck with me the whole time; even when the doctors came out of surgery and told everyone it did not go as well as they would have liked. The grim speculation from the medical specialists was we should all hope for the best and expect the worst. In their world, people did not make it many years with this kind of diagnosis. If I lived to be twenty-five it would be a surprise. That was pretty grim considering I was twenty-one when I had the surgery.

Chapter Nine

Life After Surgery

*I want to know if you can
disappoint another
to be true to yourself...*

After all of the medical treatments, weight gain and fear that goes along with this sort of experience, life isn't the same. You try to go forward but it's just different. I was unsure of what I wanted to do with my life and I felt like a stranger in my own body. I had gained a significant amount of weight and had lost a portion of my hearing. I felt scared and alone with no goal or purpose for the first time in my life.

I decided since I enjoyed cooking so much with Arthur I would go to cooking school again. My goal was to go to the Culinary Institute of America (CIA). I had dreams of creating the most amazing dishes while enjoying the entire process. I saw myself in a clean white coat and my toque learning how to cook an egg as many ways as there are folds in a toque. I may have missed my opportunity with Disney but it did not matter. I was wide-eyed and ready to start a new chapter in the culinary arts.

In order to get into CIA, I had to get some experience so I signed up for a cooking program at the local vocational. My first month in cooking school yielded finger cuts and blisters accompanied by backaches. To top it off, the vile stench of "kitchen" took permanent residence in every pore of my skin. In the first month, I peeled potatoes for an entire week. After that there was a week of cleaning grease traps and scraping scum off the floor. This was just the beginning. It was becoming very clear that this was not going to be like cooking with Arthur. There was no creativity here. This was institutional cooking and not even at its finest. Funny thing about it though, it wasn't the potatoes or layers of caked grease that got me. It was the peas.

When I finally got off of floor degreasing and potato peeling duty I was allowed to cook frozen vegetables. Yes, cook frozen veggies. This just rubbed me wrong. It defied common sense to cook something that was already cooked and these frozen veggies were already cooked. It even said so on the package. I didn't have a degree in nutrition, I didn't know much about becoming a professional chef, but I knew this was off. I finished one semester and decided vocational education was not for me. I knew what I really needed was hands-on experience. So I got a job as a Garde Manager in one of the first fusion restaurants in downtown St. Petersburg. The executive chef was a well-known one at the time and was creating a bit of excitement with her gastronomic inventions. I was so happy; it had been some time since I had something to look forward to. My plan was to get two years of kitchen experience in and then apply to CIA, while getting paid in the process. The best part? No more potatoes or cooking cooked peas. I was working with creative people, in a beautiful kitchen, at a well-known restaurant that served quality food. It only took two weeks for me to call in sick or maybe a better word was bored. I was doing what I thought I wanted, on the road to recovering my health and life and yet I still could not show up consistently for more than two weeks in a row.

Now, in the restaurant business, you don't call in sick, you work even if your skin is falling off. If you don't go to work, someone has to cover for you. This is true of all jobs, but especially in a kitchen. I only lasted a month there and I learned a valuable lesson. I learned that it's not always a good idea to turn a hobby into a profession. Just because I loved cooking with Arthur did not mean I loved it enough to do it as a profession. I was also learning that I had no real ambition or goal in life since my dream of flying above the clouds in a military fashion was now gone.

During this time, Greg was hard at work selling cars and learning he wasn't very happy either. He started to look for other possibilities and shortly after my chemotherapy and radiation treatments were over he decided that his possibility was to be found in AMWAY. AMWAY, short for American Way, was a multilevel marketing company known for their soap. After everything that had happened I was not up for another one of Greg's get rich quick schemes and I definitely did not want to participate in AMWAY, but it got even better; he also wanted to join the Army.

Greg was always looking for a short cut to his pot of gold. I admit his risk taking quality was one thing I admired about him and yet it scared me. His first get rich quick "business" venture was selling knock-off perfumes that lost him all his money. Now he wanted to join AMWAY and join the Army. He felt AMWAY was the ticket and the Army was the perfect place to meet people for his side business. I was shocked. I was more prepared for the AMWAY news than the Army news. After my surgery, I was seeing the world differently and I was opening my eyes to a new understanding about the military. My new understanding - the military owned you, they own your thoughts, and everything else about your life. Yes, I know earth shattering. I had always looked at the Army as you work your way up, be in charge and you own it, but not true. This new understanding, combined with the fear of everyday life made it hard to just breathe. I was exhausted and yet, I couldn't let Greg go. So, instead of saying, "I can't do this" I said, "Okay" and "I do". Greg was finally going to do what he loved, be a soldier.

A month after the news of his enlistment, we were married and Fred gave me away. We had a big church wedding. Family from all over came in and a lot of Mom's crafter friends attended. I had been with Greg for six years and always knew I would marry him someday. I just never counted on someday coming so soon. I loved Greg, I enjoyed his company and we had a lot of history. But, being married changed everything. Up to this point, we had experienced a lot of turmoil together. His mom and sisters didn't care for me. I had been sick and he had tried and failed at a lot of things. Looking back, it's fair to say we were kids who grew up together. Yet, what was it that held us together? I couldn't really put a finger on it and now we were married.

Greg loved being in the Army and it was the happiest I ever saw him. I continued to live in Florida. I refused to leave the area where I grew up. It just didn't feel safe to run off with my husband. Eventually, it got difficult to have two households on an Army private's salary. So, Greg got an honorable discharge from the Army. When he enlisted, the recruiters told him he would be stationed near my doctors but that never happened. I want to be very clear.

I did not ask Greg to leave the Army but, I didn't make it easy on him either.

The following year was very difficult. I was perpetually depressed and became less and less interested in being with Greg. I was riddled with symptoms and body ailments that were left over from chemo, radiation and surgery. I eventually started taking antidepressants and began seeing a counselor. I became more and more withdrawn from Greg and everything around us. He continued to build his AMWAY business. Yet, every mention of going to another seminar or selling the plan to someone made me physically ill.

It wasn't until he started a new job and met Paula, a coworker, that things really shifted. Greg was always friendly and just plain nice to everyone; he was a pleaser and a charmer. This new friend of his made me uncomfortable and right away I was on alert. She was married with two kids and talked about her husband as abusive and not so bright. Always with a criticism followed by a "poor me". I didn't like her or the way I felt when I was around her but, something about her interested Greg, so I was friendly. Very early in our friendship we got a call from her asking for help in a whisper on the phone. Her husband had lost his mind, beat her and then left. I'm not sure what it was about her, as I said I didn't like her yet I was cautiously attracted to her. Maybe it was because I was accustomed to taking care of women in distress as I had all of my life with my mom. I don't know, but something in the back of my head said keep your eye on this woman. So I did.

I don't remember a lot of the details because she confided in Greg mostly but eventually she and her husband broke up. Then, she began flirting with both Greg and me. She was reeling us both in with sexual innuendos while playing on our sympathies. When the three of us went out she would dance with me like a lover. This really turned me on and I well...I was married to Greg and wanted to be with Paula. I was in a marriage that I rarely, if ever wanted to make love to my husband, but craved the touch of a woman. I was confused and turned on all at once. I had never craved a man the way I craved this woman. I had never felt what I was feeling; all I wanted was to be with this woman. As time went on I began to drink heavily in hopes that these feelings would go away but they didn't. I began to have black outs and one morning Greg sat down with me and told me all the terrible things I did the night before when I was plastered. I was so upset the only thing I could think to do was to call Greg's Aunt Rose – the one who took him in when he was in the fragrance business. I don't know why I wanted to talk to Aunt Rose but it didn't matter, I left the house and drove to where she worked. I was distraught. I couldn't believe the things Greg told me. What was happening to me? I was depressed, drinking and my world was falling apart. Aunt Rose and I talked for a long time and she scheduled an appointment for me with a crisis center. Later that day Greg and Paula took me to the appointment. When we got to the appointment the counselor at the center informed me that I was severely depressed and that I should be admitted immediately. I had no insurance or money so that didn't happen. I left the appointment with little if any help or answers.

A few weeks passed and I found myself going over to Paula's house more often. I would take her where she needed to go, and we talked on the phone every chance we got. I was so into this feeling I didn't even notice Greg wasn't in the picture until he was gone. I remember coming home one night from working out with Paula and he told me he was moving out. I was devastated and relieved at the same time. My world was spinning and I didn't know up from down and yet there was a sense of freedom.

After Greg left, I began to drink all the time and if I was not drinking I was at Paula's house. She had no car and I was more than happy to be her chauffer. It wasn't long before I could no longer deny the truth. I was in love with a woman. I wanted to be with this woman more than anyone I had ever wanted and she was all too willing to dangle the carrot in front of my nose to get what she needed. Eventually the situation got to the point that I could no longer keep it to myself and I told her that I loved her. But once I said it, I could no longer be alive. Once I told her I began to panic. The night I finally told her I got really drunk and took a bunch of pills. I called her and said that I loved her and that I was leaving her all of my things. I expected to never wake up again. A short while later the paramedics and police showed up at my door and I was carted off to the hospital to have my stomach pumped and committed for twenty-four-hour observation.

When I was released, Paula picked me up from the hospital. She tried to console me and play the whole thing off like it was no big deal. What I mean is that she played off the overdosing as no big deal and ignored the fact I told her I loved her. She was determined to keep me as close as she could because she was in a predicament. Like I said earlier, she was originally Greg's friend from work and in an abusive relationship with two kids. She had gravitated towards Greg and his kind nature with hopes of replacing him for her husband. In truth she didn't care who had feelings for her, she just needed someone to take care of her and since Greg had left, she was stuck with me. For the next few weeks, she borrowed my car and my money. She acted like she cared for me and acted like we were best friends. That is until she hooked up with a guy she met in a bar. I remember the day I showed up to take her somewhere and she wouldn't answer the door. Instead she left her kids to play in the front yard so they could tell me, "We don't like Tracey anymore." I was crushed and I never saw Paula again.

I was alone and afraid. I was running out of places to go and places to hide. I had pushed the envelope so far open this time there was no going back. It was in this moment that I knew I had to admit I was gay because denying it was killing me.

Falling in love with this woman, admitting I was gay, and being Baker Acted all in one moment. I felt like a stranger in my own body just like I did after my brain surgery and well, like I had most of my life. Just out of alignment with me. I was coming to grips with something I buried so deep that I felt invaded by the unburying of it. I was admitting something to myself and to the world that just wasn't acceptable to admit. After being in a bi-racial relationship with Greg for nearly seven years you would think I would be okay with this but I just wasn't. It was not okay for me to be gay. After all I was in a relationship with a great guy and even though he left we could still work it out. Not to mention he stuck by me when I was sick. It was difficult to let go of this kind of commitment and admit I was living a lie and still, my life depended on it.

The reality of it was that Greg and I did not have a great relationship because I did not want to be with a man and I hated myself for that. He was beautiful, kind and everybody wanted to be his friend. Women were attracted to him and he was always getting hit on. I had him and didn't want him. For my entire life I had buried my feelings and attractions to women. My love for all of my close girlfriends, the way I felt when one of them gave me a hug or touched me on the back was more powerful than anything I had ever felt with Greg. I was aching to be me, yet terrified of what that meant.

I remember the first few days after admitting this and then dealing with the truth of it. I was talking with my mother. She took me into her room and showed me her porn stash of women. She had been attracted to women her entire life and yet never shared this with me. But now she was trying to reach out and make me understand there was nothing wrong with how I was feeling and she wanted to take control of the situation. She was a bit pissed that I overdosed and didn't want to take care of this kind of situation again. We talked about all of this for a while and then we talked about Rachel, Mom's crafting club partner.

My mom met Rachel shortly after she divorced Ron. Rachel sold water filters and was working on her boat captain licenses; she met my mother through our pool guy. Rachel came by the house one day to sell Mom a water filter and while there she and my mom began to talk about all the shells and crafts in the house. My mother explained it was all hers and she did crafts and set up clubs.

Rachel kept walking through the house saying, "I can do that; I can make that" and signed up for a club. The rest is history, from there they started more clubs and a business. Mom made crafts and Rachel located craft shows for the two of them to be in. Rachel was a nice person and there was something about her that made me feel different. She was cool, fun and liked to party. She and Mom went out and got trashed together a couple nights a week. On one of their nights out they met a couple of guys in town on vacation. One look and Rachel was in love with one of the guys. A few months later and Rachel married the guy and moved away.

The interesting thing about Rachel and me coming out is that Rachel is gay. She got married to a man, left town, but still she's gay. She's twenty-one years older than me, in fact she is four days older than my mom, and still I always felt tingly around her even when I first met her the day she came to the house to sell water filters. Rachel was the first gay woman I ever met that I really liked.

After the meeting in my mom's closet with her girl porn she told me Rachel was coming for a visit and wanted me to talk with her. Of course I said yes.

I remember the day. It was awkward but fun. We talked about silly stuff while visiting every one of her favorite restaurants up and down the beach. Rachel started in one location because she loved the appetizer there and then traveled to another because she loved the dinner there and then finished at yet another because they had the best dessert. By the end of the day, I was full and a little drunk because at each location Rachel ordered us both a rumrunner. It was a great day and eventually she asked me why I wanted to talk to her. I found this odd because my mother set the whole thing up and told Rachel everything. Eventually Rachel said, "The only reason I can imagine you would want to talk to me is because I'm different. I'm gay." I said, "Well, yes that is true." I then told her that I had always had feelings for her. The night ended with my first kiss from a woman being set-up by my mother.

Our one-day adventure was in the summer and by fall she packed up her stuff and moved back to Florida, leaving her husband and life. Sounds crazy when I tell the story and it was. Starting a relationship with someone old enough to be your mother. Someone who had been your mother's best friend for years with the subtle push from your mother, reminds me of a bad movie, and the lesbian joke about the U-Haul. "What does a lesbian bring on her second date? A U-Haul."

One day with Rachel and she brought a moving van all the way from New Hampshire. Her explanation to her husband was that she had to think and get away to find herself.   Well, she wanted to find herself and she wasn't prepared to hurt him or admit she was starting her first full-blown female relationship. She had been in many relationships with women but they or she was always married. In her mind, if you were cheating with a woman while married to a man it wasn't really cheating. I never quite got that but I have come to learn that a lot of homosexual people think that way. I think there is a level of shame that can come from admitting you're gay and it is too much for some to handle. It is just easier to hide. So, that's what a lot of gay people do. They hide.

After falling for Paula and then kissing Rachel, things were becoming clearer for me. Feelings and emotions I had hidden from others and myself all my life were now starting to surface and show me the real version of me. Not only was I becoming more clear about my life I also became more clear about who was accepting and who was not. Now I had always lived on the edge, or so I thought. I lived in the south and married a black man before bi-racial relationships were accepted. As a teenager, I thrived on accomplishing what I was told a girl could not do. So you would think that people would expect the unexpected from me. Well not this time and not about this topic. There were a few people who could not accept me being gay and one in particular was my neighbor turned close friend after my brain surgery. One day we were having a conversation about the whole situation and she just went off. I said something that was either offensive or just a bit too over the edge for her and we had a fight. The next thing I knew she was going off about how she was sick and tired of hearing about how I was gay and that she was over it. What was my problem? We never spoke again after that. She wasn't the only one. There were a few family members who felt the same way. I had a cousin on my mom's side of the family tell me if that's what I wanted then we were through. Needless to say I never spoke with that cousin again. I had spent twenty-six years in the closet and I was not going to hide any more.

Fred on the other hand was quite amazing. I called him and said, "Well, umm, well Dad, I'm gay". His response, "Okay", and that was that. Fred didn't care, he just wanted me to be happy, he wasn't crazy about Rachel he just wanted me to be happy. So to him, if this was me so be it.

Once Rachel and I got situated in her new house we opened a craft gallery and Mom moved her craft clubs to our studio. We had a really booming business and things were going well. Rachel was running the shop, I had provided Mom with a place for her clubs and still I wasn't happy. I continued to battle severe depression and started to take depression medication in addition to drinking regularly. I was no stranger to drinking. I started when I was thirteen but, this time it was different. Rachel was a heavy drinker and loved to eat. She was also an avid runner and loved to work out. I just loved to drink and eat. Over the course of our five years together, I kept gaining weight and eventually maxed out at just over two hundred and fifty pounds. Now, if that wasn't uncomfortable enough, I began to lose my hearing as a side effect of my brain tumor, the surgery, and all the harsh treatments. This was no surprise though; I was told I would lose my hearing from bone decay; a side effect of radiation. Turns out it wasn't the bones that were failing. It was a buildup of scar tissue from chemo and radiation that was creating pressure on my auditory nerves. In addition to hearing loss, my balance was severely compromised. While I proved the experts wrong by living past the age of twenty-five, I did not escape their prognosis of hearing loss and by the time I was thirty-years-old I was wearing hearing aids in both ears. It was devastating to me.

After all the effects of surgery, depression medication, drinking and a large dose of self-hate I was grinding to a halt. I was beginning to see the absurdity of my age-inappropriate relationship that mirrored my relationship with my mother. I was unhappy, unhealthy and looking for someone to fix me. It was about this time that Rachel met Maggie. Maggie was a crafter at the gallery; she was referred to us from a Chamber of Commerce connection. Maggie and Rachel hit it off immediately and Rachel asked me to go meet Maggie for lunch and find out if she was gay. Since marketing was my part of the business, I figured this would be a chance to get more connections. Plus, another friend couldn't hurt.

I met Maggie, introduced myself and began to dig for information. During lunch I learned everything I needed to know and reported back to Rachel that her "gaydar" was right on and Maggie was indeed gay. Rachel and I were happy to have a new friend and a new friend with connections never hurt, but I never saw it coming. The truth is Rachel was interested in Maggie and before I knew what was happening, Rachel told me she didn't love me anymore. She was now in love with Maggie and our relationship was over. We were together for five years and built a business together and now it was over.

My world began to spin. I was already unhappy but I loved Rachel more than words could express. I had no ability to handle this. I felt as though the air was being sucked from my lungs. I couldn't think, I couldn't breathe or see straight. Everything was blurry and I felt sick. I had no money and no job outside of our business, which at this point Rachel claimed was all hers because she invested the startup money.

Over the next few days things just felt fuzzy. The back and forth of shock and heartbreak consumed me. It wasn't until a few days later it would really hit me. We were at a business event and Maggie and Rachel were there.

It was the first time I saw them together since Rachel had dropped the bomb on me. I remember walking up to them and Rachel looked at me and said "I need to talk to Maggie alone" and asked me to leave and that was all it took. I went home, opened every bottle of pills I had, every anti-depression medication, every drug I had. I took them all and then...BOOM! The voice of GOD rang in my head, "WHAT ARE YOU DOING? GO GET HELP NOW!!!." Up 'til then, I never lead a spiritual life. My only experience with miracles and blessings were from the prayers and good thoughts I received while I was going through brain surgery and cancer treatment. Deep down I had positive, happy thoughts that felt like fairy tales, but that was it. So why did I, all of a sudden, hear it now? I don't know. But once you've downed about a thousand pills it's a little late to take it back, so I listened. I got dressed, I got in my car and heading for...I didn't really know where, I was just on the move. I think I thought if I moved fast enough away from where it all happened it would go away. The first rational thought that came to me was to call our friends Jeff and Kim. So I did.

Jeff and Kim were friends of Rachel and mine. Jeff was a bus driver with some Emergency Medical Technician (EMT) experience and Kim was a stay-at-home mom. They were kind and funny with two beautiful boys and for some reason it felt safe to call them. Once I had them on the phone they immediately offered assistance. I told them I would come right over if they promised to help me just throw up and not to call the paramedics. They agreed and I headed to their house. By the time I got there I was completely out of it and pissed because they had called the paramedics and police. I had pulled this once before and got off with a slap on the wrist. This time I knew I would be in a bigger mess. So no way did I want to go to the hospital or involve any authorities. Didn't matter, the police and ambulance were on their way and lucky for me. This time I took some serious stuff and needed to get it out.

I ended up being committed for a week in a drug and alcohol abuse program. Interesting thing was that the whole time I was there I kept insisting I had no issue with drugs. Again, I was in denial about the course of my life and the events I had allowed to unfold. I was lucky though, I could have been sent away for a long time and had who knows what done to me and given to me. The whole thing is really scary when I think about it. Lucky for me I listened to the voice telling me to get help that night. The whole time I had an Angel looking over me even though I couldn't see it.

When I got out of the hospital I went home. Let me rephrase, I went to Rachel's house. I had been living there even though she and Maggie were now dating. I didn't have anywhere to go or money to go anywhere with.

Everything I had was tied to the business and Rachel held it all. She did eventually loan me $1,000 to move out. Like everything else, she was keeping track and controlling it all. In her mind I had to pay her back the money she loaned me to move out so she could have her new girlfriend move in. The new girlfriend she originally sent me to meet and make friends with.

That was something about Rachel; she kept records of every expense and kept tabs on everything. At the time it seemed fair. I assumed keeping score was what you did. I didn't have anything of value to offer so keeping track of what I owed seemed logical at the time. Living with Rachel was like growing up with my mom, there was always a condition. If I do this, you have to do that. I can help you with this, but you owe me. The reality of it was that I was not only in a relationship with someone my mother's age; I was in a relationship with an altered version of my mother that was originally set up by my mother the day we talked about me coming out. How messed up was that? Still, I did not see it all completely.

Chapter Ten

On My Own

I want to know if you can see Beauty
even when it is not pretty
every day...

I was on my own; no job, no partner and no feeling of self-worth. I was morbidly obese and unhappy, strung out on depression medication and feeling worse every day. I can't think of anything that made me happy during this time. I cleaned houses and offices for a living and considered it a loser job. Even though I paid my bills and got by, I did not see myself as blessed or lucky to be alive. Instead I focused more on the fact that I felt like my body was failing and that I was alone. I continued to experience hearing loss. I seldom dated and only had one semi-serious relationship during this time. With the mental and physical state I was in it was understandable. I would not have wanted to date me during this time either.

Eventually I did date and even lived with a woman named Beverly. Beverly was interesting; she was telepathic and incredibly intuitive. She also suffered from obsessive-compulsive disorder and had been severely abused as a child. Her gift was a survival tool that helped her navigate the world around her and discern what was and was not safe. I could relate to her in more ways than I liked to admit. She was kind and quirky; more interested in having a friendship than a relationship. I never quite believed her when she told me she could hear thoughts until one day we were in the grocery store. I was looking for and thinking, "Where is the toothpaste with fluoride?" The next thing I knew she came around the corner and said, "Why do you want fluoride?" as though we were discussing toothpaste options. I was looking for fluoride toothpaste yet I never said a word about it out loud. She was also good at pointing out how much mind chatter I had going on. She would tell me to stop and be quiet even when I wasn't talking. I believe I met Beverly so that she could show me a world outside of my black and white view. Beverly was one of the first people to show me that there is more going on than what you can see or touch. It wasn't obvious to me then but now I understand the purpose of that relationship. Beverly was another one of the many messengers who showed up just at the right time in my life. She stepped on the stage, played her part, and then exited exactly as scripted.

Eventually I broke up with Beverly because she was incapable of sharing intimacy or having a deep relationship with anyone other than her little poodle. It is my belief that all of the abuse she experienced as a child left her too guarded and full of fear to really open up to someone else.

After I broke up with Beverly I had to move again and I had to get ready for a visit from Fred. Every winter Fred came down and visited me. I can't imagine what he thought. The numerous times I moved and the women I dated. All the while he just smiled and passed no judgment. Fred was a great friend who understood me better than I understood myself. I remember one year he came down to visit and that after one day I got antsy and panicky. I explained what I was feeling. He instantly knew what I was feeling and offered to leave the next day. I didn't have to say to him I was freaking out because he was in my space. He just knew and was okay with it. He understood it was about me and not him. He also experienced the same anxiety and panic moments and understood what I was going through.

◆ ◆ ◆

During this time I made it a point to see my mother at least once a week. I kept in contact with her out of obligation and to be sure she was okay. I was still playing the role of caretaker that was laid on me at the age of three; even though I didn't see it that way at the time. Around this time, she met a guy named Bob. She was just getting over an unhealthy relationship with a much younger and abusive guy so Bob was a big improvement. She eventually married him and I was genuinely happy for her. The way I looked at it was that Bob took some of that caregiving obligation off me.

Shortly after her wedding we had our first conversation where I actually stood up for myself. I stopped by her house for something; I can't remember what, and she started in on me about the student loan she took out for me. The student loan that paid her back property taxes and some living expenses while I was in school. She told me it was a serious matter and I needed to handle it. I told her there was no way I could pay it now but if she paid the part she owed, I would take over payments once her portion was paid off. This pissed her off beyond belief and she used every trick in the book to get me to do what she wanted, to pay it all. I looked at her and said "no" and walked away. Before this moment I had never said no to my mother and I don't know why I picked this issue to start but I did. To my surprise, she followed me out the door and completely changed the subject. It was a shocking moment. I had never stood up to her and she had never back off so quickly.

◆ ◆ ◆

Between Fred coming and going the next day, and Mom getting married I started to surf the Internet looking for anything that would ease the loneliness I was feeling. I started to search for information but kept being called to books of a spiritual nature.

I read Marianne Williamson, Neal Donald Walsh and Iyanla Vanzant. I loved Miguel Ruiz', *The Four Agreements*. I was hooked on spiritual information and the mind body connection. I couldn't explain it. I didn't understand most of it and didn't live or practice any of it yet, I could feel the connection to it deep inside of me starting to wake up. I would catch a conversation here or read something there, remember something Beverly said or recalled a line in a book I had read. I was being reminded over and over in subtle ways that everything was connected and possibility lived in it all.

In the back of my mind I always knew that anything was possible and had amazing reminders of this truth. The fact that I was still alive and only suffered hearing loss from a life-threatening tumor. Or thinking back to when I was in high school and I decided I was going to Europe and fly gliders. And I did. I just knew if I put my mind to it I could do it. I was beginning to see what could be and I was seeing what had come to pass. At that moment in my life, my body and my environment were not very supportive of these insights. I had not lived in alignment with my possibilities, but I was starting to. As I continued to read and search for more information I began to find me.

Just as I was starting to find me, Rachel and Maggie began to have relationship issues. Maggie had received a large inheritance and wanted to invest in a business so she thought it would be cool to buy a deli in a very wealthy part of town. When Maggie started her business she began to experiencing all sorts of new pressures and making new acquaintances in the process. Everything was changing for her and I could never understand what attracted her to the food business. After my restaurant and culinary adventure with the vocational school, I stayed as far away as I could from the food industry. Still, I was a sucker for helping those who didn't need help and since I was still friends with them I offered to help. For some reason I just had this thing about helping those who had done me wrong. What was my reason for being a sucker this time? I still cared for Rachel and still wanted to be involved in her life. It was interesting spending that much time around Maggie. She was a nice person and the more I worked with her the more I genuinely liked her. The more I liked her as a friend the more I noticed she and Rachel weren't getting along too well. Along with this new business endeavor came the need for a few employees so I got my mom's daughter-in-law, Janice, a job at the deli. Janice eventually let me in on a little secret. Maggie was seeing someone behind Rachel's back.

I was shocked and then I remembered something my mom had told me when I was drowning in my tears over Rachel. She said, "Rachel is a five-year commitment and that's it, Maggie and Rachel won't last." At the time, it made me feel better but now I was thinking, how did she know that? Regardless, she was right. But this time it wasn't Rachel ending it; it was Maggie. Usually Rachel was the one leaving one relationship for another and now for the first time in her life it was happening to her. She was the one being left and I knew she would be heart broken. And she was.

It was a Sunday afternoon and the three of us were having lunch and I began to tell a story of how I had a friend and I knew her partner was cheating on her. I asked them "What would you do? Do you tell the friend or do you just keep your mouth shut?" The general consensus was say nothing. Later that week I got a phone call from Rachel asking me if the friend was her and I said "yes".

Apparently, Maggie started coming home very late. The night Rachel called me Maggie didn't come home at all. Rachel was a mess. Like I said, she never had anyone she cared about leave her. In the next few weeks, Rachel packed Maggie's things and she was gone. Maggie didn't even go home to pack her own things, I helped Rachel pack them. Life is not without irony and while I wish I could say I felt bad for Rachel, I didn't. I was happy I was there to help her and be the shoulder to cry on. In the back of my mind I was thinking, "About how long will it take for her to be over this one and want me back?"

Chapter Eleven

Here We Go Again!

It doesn't interest me
if the story you are telling me
is true...

In time, Rachel and I became better friends; we spent most weekends together and talked all the time. We even planned to move to another state together.

Somewhere along the line we got this bright idea that we should move to Ashville, North Carolina together...as friends. I thought, great, I loved that area and if Rachel wanted to have me come along I'm there. We took a trip to the area and scoped out the place. We hooked up with a Realtor who was connected to the gay and lesbian community and planned to move there in March of 2008. Everything was set and I was excited to be going on a new adventure and starting a whole new life. Even though I didn't see that I was taking the same old baggage with me.

The month before we were scheduled to leave was February and both of our birthdays so our friends planned a birthday/going away party. Let me rephrase that. My friends threw us a party. This time around I started to notice some things differently. I started to notice Rachel didn't have a lot of her own friends and only made friends when we were together. My friends had become her friends. I also started to notice how people interacted with her. She was kind of a social Neanderthal. Now I know that sounds harsh and, well, I guess it is. Rachel did not possess many social graces. People didn't always get her awkward way and because of that she had a difficult time in social settings. The truth is I started the conversations and made the connections. Even when we were in business together, I was the one pounding the pavement making a name for our craft gallery. It was me who went out and made friends with Maggie while Rachel was behind the scenes running the shop. This was an earth shaking realization and it hit me hard, as most realizations of conscious and shifting proportions do. Yet, I still planned to move away with her, give up my cleaning business, and follow her into the mountains.

It was at our, (my), going away party that Jane, one of our friends, invited me to the big lesbian Valentine's Day dance with her the week before we were leaving. I was ecstatic. I had not been out on a date in ages and Jane was a well-known character in my circle of friends. She was my perfect type, too old and too drunk, too much of the time. For years she had owned a thriving upscale spa in town and was considered a big catch in the lesbian community. Currently, she was not working or running her spa. The only thing she was working on these days was sucking in her next victim. Jane was the type you might call the "un-getable" get. You know the type. The one who's aloof and distant, who doesn't show enough interest, but just enough to hook you and drag you along for miles. I didn't see any of it, I was just excited to be invited to the party by the girl who no one could get. This really annoyed Rachel because she felt Jane should be interested in her. That and the fact that Jane was "well to do" didn't hurt. I think it was the "well to do" that really got Rachel's attention though.

As things were winding down and we were packing for our move, I was planning for this date. I had moved back in with Rachel out of convenience for the move and to save some money. The money saving didn't happen because Rachel charged me rent for the two months I was there. But, back to my date. Jane picked me up and we were off. It was a great time and I felt like magic was in the air. I had not felt this amazing in years. Someone was interested in me and did not care that I was overweight or that I couldn't hear most of what was being said. I had been single and sexless for five years and finally someone wanted me.

Jane was incredible and made me feel special. Our date turned into a week of dates, dinners, and more. It was the most amazing time I had ever had. On the night before I was to leave, we laid in bed together and she promised to visit and wished I wouldn't go. Now I didn't hear most of what was said in those days but I heard that. She said she wished I wasn't leaving and she would visit me. I said, "Wait a minute! Did you just say you wished I wouldn't go?" She said, "That's what I said!" I looked at her and said, "Well then I can't go." She rolled over and laughed and said "I'd like to see you pull this off." The next day I told Rachel I wasn't going and we had to unpack the truck.

Remember the lesbian joke, "What does a lesbian bring on the second date? A U-Haul. Well I brought the U-Haul, unpacked my stuff and repacked Rachel's stuff in Jane's front yard. I filled her garage and moved into the second floor of her four-story home. She was on the fourth floor and I was on the second floor and I didn't care. I was in love. For the next month we cocooned. We went nowhere and just spent time together. It was amazing and when I told my mother she was pissed. In her mind getting rid of me to another state was a relief. Not to mention, she loved North Carolina and was planning to vacation there a few months a year as she would have a free place to stay. At one time she had a cabin in the Ashville area she could not afford to keep. So me moving away was great, she would have a free place to stay and I would be gone, available only by phone call for what she needed and when she needed it. The day I called her and told her I was not moving, she screamed and yelled at me on the phone, "I can't believe how you are fucking up your life!" She was pissed and we didn't talk for six months after that.

Fred on the other hand was much better at handling these things, he simply said, "Well okay." By this time in our relationship, he never knew what he was going to get with a phone call from me. "Hello Fred, I'm dating a black guy." "Hi Fred, I have a brain tumor." "Fred...I'm gay and dating someone as old as my mother." He just rolled with the punches. I think he was just glad that I had not decided to date a goat, although he probably would have been fine with that too.

Jane was very into holistic healing and was spiritual in her own right. One of the first things she did was to hook me up with a friend of hers from her old spa who was an Ayurvedic doctor. The Ayurvedic doctor worked on my hearing, balance and overall mental state. It was very interesting. Every day I showed up for an oil dripping treatment that dripped oil slowly and directly into my third eye. The entire experience, as strange as it seemed, was very healing. It opened me up and created a space for me to find my voice. At the time I didn't see it that way. But as the next few months began to unfold, I couldn't deny the shift.

After a month, things began to unravel. I was no longer welcome in Jane's bedroom and she was never home. I was trying to rebuild my cleaning business since I had given all my accounts away because I was moving. I had depleted my moving funds and was beginning to get nervous. It was a non-stop drinking scene and Jane even slept with a drink beside her bed. She avoided me and there was a constant flow of people coming in and out of her house. She even had a boyfriend or just, friend, this was never clear, in prison who was about to get out of jail and move into the first floor of her house. I was starting to see I was in a place I had no business being in. It reminded me of being a child. Always someone drunk and always eggshells to navigate around in an attempt to find safety. Everything was a wreck and I was scared and lonely. It felt like I had no one. I was in desperate need of someone to talk to so I called Greg's Aunt Rose and asked if I could come for a visit. She could tell by the tone of my voice it was serious and in true Aunt Rose fashion she was more than happy to have me come for a visit. I drove up to see her and remember the minute I got out of the car she hugged me and I began to cry. Without question or judgment she said, "Talk to me, what's going on?" We talked for hours and she just listened and loved me right where I was in that moment, offering only compassion and positive input. I could always count on Aunt Rose to help me find the light.

When I got back from visiting Aunt Rose I knew I had to move out of Jane's and by the end of April, I was in my own apartment. This time I had really pushed the envelope to extremes. In fact, I don't think there was even a fold left. I was wide open and hanging on by a fine thread. My rent was $500.00 a month and I only made $200.00. I worked around the clock to get more business and then I worked even harder, cleaning for anyone who would hire me. And if this wasn't enough to keep me on my toes, one morning I woke up and had completely lost all of my hearing. I could hear nothing and I mean nothing. I was totally cut off from everything. I couldn't even hear the usual ringing in my ears that had been there since forever. It was all gone. I was in a state of total panic. I immediately made an appointment with my audiologist and their neurologist. The only thing they could come up with was that I had fluid in my ears so they gave me steroids and sent me on my way. While it was true the fluid in my head had gotten so bad that when I rolled over in bed at night I could feel it move from one side to the other. But it never made my hearing worse. The stress of everything was taking a toll on my body and my body was talking back. My body had decided that at that moment it did not want to hear any more of this chaos I had created.

I have to admit my life was quite a mess. My only friend, Rachel, had moved away and my mother would not speak to me. I had no one or so, I thought. I was slowly approaching forty and felt like I was in a continuous downward spiral. I had nearly died three times in my life. I woke up every day wondering why I was still here and what I was supposed to be doing with my life.

Months passed and I began to shift. I started losing weight and I started to find myself. I also started to get some of my hearing back. I was still barely making enough money to pay the bills but, somehow it always worked out. During this time I never missed a payment on anything. I didn't have a lot but I learned you didn't need a lot. I had my two cats that had been with me since forever and we were brushing off the dust and beginning to see light at the end of the tunnel that gave me hope and a new perspective. I no longer felt like a victim. I was shifting my approach to life and was beginning to live life from a place of accountability. I knew I put myself here and I knew I could get myself out. That and the fact I didn't have time to feel sorry for myself. I had bills to pay and two four-legged kids to keep in cat chow and litter.

During this time I continued to turn to spirituality, as there was nothing else left to turn to. I had tried it all: sickness, relationships, drama, self-abuse, abuse from others and now I was empty. The rubber was hitting the road. I searched the Internet night after night reading more books and finding all the spiritual information I could. Each piece of information I found was a new tool that led me to search more. Finally, when I thought I had searched and found it all a whole new piece of the puzzle appeared and nothing could have prepared me for it...

Chapter Twelve

Awakening to Possibility

I want to know
if you can live with failure
yours and mine
and still stand at the edge of the lake
and shout to the silver of the full moon,
"Yes."...

I had tried many things. I read books, attended seminars and spontaneously gave my life away as I knew it. Yet nothing prepared me for the book I was about to receive. It was a book about the law of attraction. I know it sounds really hard to believe that a book would change your life, but it did. When I found it online I remember going back and forth for about two days before ordering it. It cost $14.95 plus shipping and at that time it was crazy for me to spend that kind of money on a book. That $14.95 plus shipping was a big chunk out of my grocery budget; but I didn't care. I decided I would eat less that week.

I remember the moment it arrived in the mail. As I un-wrapped it, I could feel it vibrating in my hands. I headed out to the community pool and began reading. I hadn't finished reading two paragraphs when I began to cry. It said, "Here it is, look no farther. No need for any more classes or seminars because this is everything you need to know about how to make life work." I began crying and immediately looked for a phone number to call and asked how they could say this. How could they make such claims, such big promises filled with pie in the sky that you never get to taste? The excitement was more than I could stand and the fear of what if it was a lie reminded me of AMWAY. It didn't matter, I wanted to know how I could make this work for me.

I had lived my life being filled with "shoulds" that were drowning me. What should I think, who should I love and how should I live? Did the writers of this book actually mean for me to give up the influence of someone else's expert opinion and have my own? My whole life until now was about living to please someone else. But now it was coming to an end. It was time. The divine moment I had been waiting for was at hand and it started by stepping into my possibility and potential. It was called *Law of Attraction* and I was about to learn how to use it.

I think it took a week for me to read the book the first time. I hung onto every word and began to practice its principles. I started by releasing all of the imposed ideas and thoughts of what I had been taught during my life and began to ask better questions of myself. I began to look at my life as a series of valuable learning experiences rather than a continuum of repetitive failures. I drew from the experiences and began, for the first time in my life, to get a glimpse of what I wanted, what I really wanted for my life. I began to be more conscious and purposeful about my choices, thoughts and actions. I started by being clear about what I chose to have happen rather than focusing on what I wanted to go away or change. I focused on exactly how much money I chose to earn, what kind of business I wanted and most importantly I was detailed about the partner with whom I wanted to spend the rest of my life.

Don't misunderstand me. This was hard; I had never done anything like this before. I mean, taking time to invest in me. Asking "me" what I wanted. It was difficult to look at my life this way and until this moment it never occurred to me I had a choice or that it would help to do so. I always thought I had to make myself fit into someone else's vision of me. I thought it was my job in life to make other people's opinion mine and live according to what made others comfortable. And like squeezing a watermelon through a keyhole, I had been determined to make me fit. Not any more. This time around I dared to be my own creation and I started my attracting by writing my choices down.

I started by writing down and guess what? The things I wrote down began to appear. For starters, I always had just enough money to pay all of the bills, well sometimes not quite enough, but it always worked out. During this time I learned to be more respectful with my money and to honor the abundance I was receiving. It was not a lot of money nor was it how I hoped to live the rest of my life. However, for the first time in my life, I saw and felt the magic of appreciating where I was and what I had rather than focusing on what was missing. In addition to monetary abundance I was working when and where I wanted to for people who appreciated me and what I did for them. *Law of Attraction* really was magic and I was beginning to see how it was always here and had always been here. It was just waiting for me to turn it on.

Things were beginning to get better, but I still had a lot of work to do. I was still alone and lonely. I wanted to find a partner and friend. I wanted to find my soulmate, the one, who was out there wanting to find me. I was ready to start living life and being in a career I was proud of and passionate about that helped others in a positive way. I was still searching and with every bit of inspiration and insight came answers that led to more questions. I was doing the work and it was leading to a completely new path.

The more I studied and searched, the more things started to shift and the more I wrote things down. I began to write down with clarity exactly what my partner would be like; I asked for a beautiful life partner, my soul mate, someone who would love and honor me as I would honor and love them. I declared the reason for wanting this was because I deserved it and it was my time. I had tried everything else and catered to others and now it was my turn. I had done the work and I was ready to share joy and experience joy. I wanted to be loved and acknowledged. To have a special someone in my life, to feel and to share passion and intimacy, to have someone hold my hand and appreciate me for who I was as much as I appreciated them. To give to another without being taken, and the list went on. I was done with dating age-inappropriate alcoholics and women with a fear of intimacy. I was done and I deserved more. My beautiful four-legged children deserved more and we were going to make the changes necessary to get what we chose. And it wasn't just about the partner; I was ready to be healthy and open to hear what the world had to say to me. I was ready to step into my health again and become reacquainted with my beautiful body that had been through so much and still served me so well. I was ready for a career that embraced my desire to help others. The more I searched the more I learned that my desire was to help others by teaching them about natural health and wellness. To tap into the quantum possibility that was out there waiting for them. I was ready!!!

I wrote all of this down on September 2, 2008. I read what I wrote daily to remind me of my choice to embrace this change. Every day I read the pages and knew that was my truth even though I didn't see it yet. When I got discouraged I stopped and told myself: "You're not where you're going and you're not where you have been. Be here now and know your truth."

After doing this religiously, something interesting started to happen. I began to get more cleaning accounts and actually had a little extra money each month. I started to find information about schools and programs that taught alternative medicine programs and began to receive information about different energy healing modalities. I started to learn more about quantum physics and quantum entanglement. I began to see more clearly the connection and direction that all of these events were leading me in. Each Sunday morning over bagels and coffee I would meet with the new friends I was making and we would talk about creating the life we wanted and the philosophy of change it required. For the first time ever I was starting to be, well, the only word I could come up with was happy. I was happy for the first time in my entire adult life. I was really happy, things weren't perfect, and yet I was happy. It was an odd feeling, for me but I went with it. I cried less and laughed more. I enjoyed being on my own and making decisions based on what I wanted. I was 38 years old, completely alone, and completely happy.

Chapter Thirteen

When The Moon Shines

I want to know
if you can be alone
with yourself
and if you truly like
the company you keep
in the empty moments....

In the face of this newfound happiness I started to make new friends and live my life in a whole new way. I began living in the possibility of the things I had written down. I found a couple of schools I wanted to attend and I was keeping busy with work. I also found my moonbeam or rather she found me.

Like I said, I was making friends and keeping busy. My date card was beginning to dust off and I was meeting women and going on dates. I was still hanging out with older women, but they were nice and provided friendship and conversation. I had no plans to date any of them.

It was the beginning of October and time for the yearly fall picnic just north of where I lived. It was a big event and normally well attended so I decided to go. When I got there I walked around for a while and visited with a few people and then I saw her, this gorgeous woman on a Harley. She was not too feminine and not too butch just that perfect in between with a bit of a brooding attitude. I was on my way to go over and talk to her about her motorcycle when a couple I had met the week before called me over to sit with them. Charlotte and Susan were very friendly and went out of their way to include people in their group. They introduced me to everyone and I sat down and visited for a while. Eventually the brooding woman with the Harley made her way over. She was pleasant and we visited for a while then she got up to leave and I asked her if she would give me a ride on her bike. She laughed a little and said "Whenever you want" and walked off. After she left, I sat and visited a while longer and this woman named Andrea came over to me. She said "I have a Harley, I will give you a ride whenever you like" and gave me her number and asked for mine. I kind of blew her off but said okay knowing I never intended to call her or let along ride with her. Andrea was very nice and we visited on and off for the rest of the day but all I could think about was what I would say when I called the brooder.

I called the brooder and Andrea. I never heard back from the brooder, but I did hear back from Andrea. In fact, she left me multiple messages saying "Hi! I'm the cute and adorable one from the picnic, when do you want to go for a motorcycle ride?" She left three messages before the end of the next day and by Wednesday of that week we had three dates scheduled.

Our first date was on her motorcycle. Now in theory, this was a great idea until I'm on the back of the bike and I have to wrap my arms around a woman I don't really know. I admit I didn't think this one out. She picked me up and we went to dinner and then we walked by the water. It was a perfect date and I was a perfect bitch. I completely blew her off and treated her like I was above it all. The whole time she was just as sweet as could be, doing pretty much whatever I wanted. She dropped me off and that was that until our next date.

Our second date was to go to the local jazz holiday after we had dinner at my favorite beach restaurant, Frenchy's. I was a little more excited about this date, I loved jazz and it was stone crab season. I think I love stone crab more than jazz. When we got to the restaurant she ordered everything I liked and by the time I finished my soup I was sick. I wasn't used to eating so much. I lived on a budget and juiced the majority of my meals so all this food was more than I could handle and I was done for the evening before the evening got started.

We didn't make it to the jazz holiday that evening, but we did make it to my living room sofa where we sat and talked the rest of the evening. I learned she had been nervous to go out on a date with me and had planned the entire evening around my singles profile I had online. She even did a test drive to my house before our first date to be sure she knew where she was going and to know how much time she needed to get there. She had taken the time to learn about me and was even learning sign language so she could talk with me if I could not understand what she was saying. I learned a lot about Andrea that evening. She told me she had been in a ten-year relationship with a woman and the woman cheated on her with a co-worker. I learned her mother lived with her and suffered from Alzheimer's. I also learned she was a beautiful soul who was genuine and kind. It was beautiful evening and I was completely dazzled and not so sure, all at once, so I gave her my litmus test. A poem by Oriah Mountain Dreamer called "The Invitation". I remember the first time I read it and how it made me ache for a partner and then cry. It spoke to me on so many levels and reminded me of what I had written when I was choosing what I wanted for my life. After reading it I knew if I could find someone who was as touched by the poem as I had been, I had met a potential partner. I gave her the poem and within minutes she began to cry. It was then I knew I had to stop pushing this one away and give her a chance.

In the next few days we began to talk more about ourselves. I told her my story about almost moving to North Carolina and how I fell so hard for Jane. We both laughed about it for two reasons: one, because if I had not fallen for Jane I would have moved away and we would never have met, and two, because she was originally from North Carolina. Andrea was amazing; I had never met anyone like her. She gave without attachment and continually told me "this is a gift you owe me nothing". She did this because it was who she was but she wanted to be certain I understood she was not keeping track like my ex, Rachel or my mother, who calculated everything and kept a running tab. I began to really like her and how it felt to be spoiled. She did thoughtful things like take me grocery shopping or buy me simple things I needed. No one had ever done that for me before.

I was getting everything I had asked for and by the end of the second month, I started to panic. I called her one day and said, "We're going too fast I'm not sure I can do this." I was scared and I intended to break up with her that day. Her response was, "No worries, let's talk about it. I will come by after work." I couldn't believe what I was hearing. "Let's talk about it?" I wasn't sure what to do with that and all I remember thinking is "Oh My God, I want this one. She's the ONE!!!" When she got to my house I open the door naked...not completely naked, I had leather motorcycle chaps on, and nothing else. Her eyes popped wide open and I said "We still have to take it slow."

Over the next few months it was amazing how things just fell into place. Andrea was everything I had asked for in a partner. When I went back and looked over what I had written down only two months earlier I was even more dazed by what I had created by tapping into the universal law of attraction. This beautiful soul had answered my prayers and showed up exactly like I had asked. We took it slow and just had a lot of fun and since her mother lived with her this prevented us from falling into the dreaded "U-Haul syndrome" that lesbians are famous for like I did with Jane. Andrea's mom was a blessing to have around and it gave us time to get to know each other and to completely heal from the hurt we had both just experienced.

We had so much fun whenever we were together. I met all of her friends and they were just as fun as her, and they all had nice things to say about Andrea in front of and behind her back. We had a great time everywhere we went. I remember one of our dates in those first months was a psychic fair. Andrea wasn't as into spirituality, alternative medicine or law of attraction as I was but that didn't stop her from going to those kinds of things with me. At the psychic fair she decided to be brave with me. We had a reading done together. The man who did the reading told us we were old souls and this was not our first lifetime together. He also said I was the sun and she was the moon and that she would gravitate towards me. We laughed about that and agreed. From that moment on I called her my moonbeam and she called me the sun.

It wasn't long after I met Andrea that my mother decided to start talking to me again. She was over being angry with me for "fucking up my life" and the disappointment of losing her free place to stay in the mountains was fading.

Andrea was happy about this development and more than eager to meet her and just like she spoiled me, she spoiled my mother whenever she was around. We would do holidays and dinner once a month and Andrea was always generous. My mother liked Andrea and Andrea liked her. When Fred came down that year to visit he fell in love with Andrea. I had never been so happy and Fred noticed right away.

About six months later Andrea's mom decided to moved back to North Carolina and Andrea and I decided to move in together. In addition to moving in together I was starting school. I had found a school that offered a degree in alternative medicine and I signed up. It was exciting and I couldn't believe I was going to go to school to study something I had become so passionate about. I had to pinch myself because everything I had written down was now coming true. I was in a relationship. I was going to school to study what I wanted to do. And to top it all off, I was happy. I was living and receiving everything I had asked for and chosen. My possibility was showing up.

Chapter Fourteen

Moon Beam and Sunshine

I want to know
what you ache for
and if you dare to dream
of meeting your heart's longing...

School was everything I had hoped it would be. But, it was hard. I could not hear most of what was being said in class. I recorded a four-hour class and then came home and had Andrea listen to the class and take notes on it for me. I then spent a couple more hours re-doing the class and going over what I missed. It was a huge amount of effort and it was fun. I learned so much and met some amazing people. I began to think even further outside of the box I had built and was seeing possibilities I never imagined. I wanted to go to school and learn about an alternative way to heal and be healthy. I had been so sick and unhappy most of my life. I survived an illness that statistically should have killed me and lived years being depressed and morbidly obese under the supervision of allopathic medicine. I knew there was a better way and the more I learned the more I grew. The more I struggled to hear in the classroom the more determined I was. I felt like a teenager again excited about the thought of soaring above the clouds.

After all the classes and lessons, I started to understand it wasn't about allopathic or naturopathic healing. It wasn't one way or the other. I began to see that living healthy meant you had to be open to change when it was needed, and be willing to maintain when things worked. I learned that living and being healthy meant you had to be accountable and take charge of your health and your thoughts. You had to be willing and brave enough to be your own personal expert. You had to take the time to listen to yourself and trust the information you were receiving because *you knew you better* than anyone else's expert diagnosis. Don't get me wrong, there is a time and place for everything. If you get in a car accident and have broken bones go get help now, but if you have a nondescript illness and want to ask the expert about how to fix you, you will be in for a not-so-fun adventure.

Going to school was the best thing I had ever done for myself. It was the learning platform I needed to create the next step in my journey. Not only was I having fun learning, I was actually enjoying my life and I was in love with Andrea and she was in love with me. I knew she was the one. She loved the poem and passed all three of her ninety-day probation periods. The only thing left to do was to ask her to marry me and I did. She said, "Yes" and the next year we had a commitment ceremony offici- ated by a shaman. Our wedding invitations had the poem I gave Andrea to read when we met on the front, "The Invitation" by Oriah Mountain Dreamer and Aunt Rose read the poem at the ceremony. It was a beautiful event attended by approximately one hundred family members and closest friends. Fred even came from Michigan. I was really touched at the amount of help and blessings we received. It was a happy and fun ceremony, anything but conventional. People still tell us today that it was an awe- some time and we should do it again.

After the wedding and my excitement from being in school, a new dynamic began to play out with my moth- er. Well, maybe not a new dynamic but instead the be- ginning of the end. One afternoon, Andrea and I went to see my mom. She had gotten new furniture and wanted us to see it. We hung around for about a half an hour when she said she wanted to show Andrea and me a new crafting project she had been working on. What she really wanted to do was confront me in front of Andrea. She showed us the project and then started to talk about the parent loan that was taken out to pay for her property taxes years ago.

This is the same conversation we had had before when I told her that if she would pay her portion of the loan I would take over the payments once she had paid her part. She never did; she just kept deferring the loan. This had been a point of contention with us in the past, and yet here I was again telling her to pay back her part and I would get the rest. The same conversation, only this time she brought it up in front of Andrea and I wasn't going to stand for it. I knew her reason for bringing it up. Her plan was to get Andrea to pay it or have Andrea get me to pay it.

I looked at Andrea and asked her to leave the room. I then looked at my mother and fell into the old pattern of squabbling with her. I even reminded her of how she told me she wished she never had me. Her response was to mock me and make fun it a taunting voice. It was at that moment I stopped. I looked her in the eyes, held her hands and said, "I love you. I can't do this with you anymore," and walked out of her house.

That's the last time I spoke to my mother. Even today we do not speak and it's a blessing. I'm very clear that I love her and I'm very clear that I don't like a lot about her. I now understand I am not required to have both like and love for my mother. I understand I can just love her because she is a person and not just because she is my mother. I also understand that it's not my job to take care of her anymore. The first time she asked me to take care of her was when I was three and we were at Sleeping Bear Dunes. It was inappropriate and it was not fair and I really don't think she mean it how I heard it. Well maybe she did, but that doesn't mean it was my job or that it was an appropriate thing to ask of a three-year-old, but she didn't know any better. She was doing the best she could to get through her six bad months so she could find a glimpse of happiness in her six good months and standing in her studio that day I finally got it. I finally saw that she was the child and I was the caretaker and she was never going to grow up. She was never going to stop expecting me to take care of her. It was in that moment I finally understood that there was no real love being served at her table and that I had the right to get up and leave. So I did.

Chapter Fifteen

Back To Where We Started

I want to know
if you will risk
looking like a fool
for love
for your dream
for the adventure of being alive...

What is it about family that can rock you to your core? I mean really? I have always looked at people as being connected and yet when it came to family, I didn't feel connected. I had no understanding nor had I ever experienced a family connection, but I was about to.

Fred, my dad, was in the hospital again and after a year of the worst health he had experienced ever, it wasn't looking good. I knew the last time I saw him, about a year earlier, there was a strong possibility I may not see him alive again. I had been preparing for it and in the back of my mind knew what was coming. He had been in and out of the hospital several times in the past few months and to be honest I was expecting a phone call any day. Linda, his wife, was keeping me informed and I found it a little uncomfortable to be relying on her for information. Yet, there was not a whole lot I could do unless I was willing to fly up and see first-hand. It finally got to the point that I knew I needed to go. As I booked my ticket I remember thinking about my cousin's comments on how our family was great at pulling together in a crisis. That comment and having to rely on Linda left me less than thrilled about the trip. Even harder than that, I knew I was going to say good-bye to my dad.

I was scheduled to spend Thursday through Sunday in Michigan. I was going to stay at a special residence for people from out of town with family members in the hospital, a facility similar to hospice. I was nervous and not sure of what to expect once I got there so the Sunday afternoon before my trip, Andrea and I went downtown to visit one of our favorite places to eat with Dad. We sat across from the beautiful banyan trees I loved and watched people walk by. We just sat. I felt like Dad was everywhere. He loved this spot and when he came down to visit we always sat here and people watched. Dad had a knack for attracting the strangest people no matter where he went. It was something we all teased him about and said he had a weirdo magnet. As Andrea and I sat there enjoying the view, a raven landed and walked around our feet for a long while. It was beautiful and proud with all of its colors glistening in the sun and as quickly as it appeared it was gone. I knew right then Dad had transitioned. And later that evening I got the call.

Linda and Brittany, my half-sister, picked me up at the airport. They were very nice and told me about the arrangements. My only request was that I wanted to get up and say something at the ceremony. They had no problem with that.

The next day at the funeral home, I spoke with the minister about saying something at the end. He informed me I would not be allowed to speak because he was carrying out my father's wishes by giving his sermon only. He then asked me about my faith, and if I believed in God. He wanted to know about my husband and how I lived my life. I was pissed. On top of having to deal with my dad's death I had to deal with this asshole. I thought about it all night. The next morning before the funeral I told the minister there was no way he knew my father's wishes better than me and if we were in his church he could tell me not to speak. But, not in the funeral home and also that my life was of no concern to him. As I sat in the room listening to the minister quote bible verses and preach his text sermon I was more determined than ever to get up and speak. I began to get nervous and my heart started to race. Who was I to get up and speak and then all of a sudden a calm came over me and I heard a voice tell me to breathe. The voice reminded me that I had my entire family sitting behind me and if I wanted to get up and speak I should. I was told that this moment would not happen again and that I did not have to miss a chance to say goodbye to my dad because of a religious "minister" and his judgments of me. When he finished I raised my hand, just like in school, I wanted to be polite and give him the chance to call me up. Instead he just walked out of the room. As he exited I got up and walked to the podium and said what I had to say. I heard the voice of God that day and I listened. I stepped into what I was called to do and I found my voice. I said goodbye to my dad and reminded everyone that he was and always will be a part of us. I felt proud and I felt complete.

In living, Dad gave what he was capable of giving. But, more importantly, he loved me and left me with a big surprise. A family. As a result of the conversation I had with my cousin a few days before the funeral she rallied my aunts and cousins together and the Sunday after the funeral we all gathered around my Aunt Cynthia's table. They were all there and ready to hear what I had to say. I told them everything about growing up and what my life was like. I told them how I felt like the kid that fell between the cracks, the one who no one ever had time for or even cared if they did have time. They heard me and allowed me to speak. When I finished talking, I looked to my left and asked "Who is the extra plate for?" They answered, "That's where your dad is sitting." I was finally heard and in that moment, I was transformed, I was allowed to heal. It was beautiful and I will never forget it.

Flying home the next day, as I sat on the plane, I felt complete. I felt grateful. I felt whole.

Chapter Sixteen

It's All Connected

I want to know
if you can be with joy
mine or your own
if you can dance with wildness...

After everything was said and done, my dear friend and surrogate mom, Kayla, and I were talking about my mom and dad and how I grew up. She reminded me that the people who treat you the worst are the ones who love you the most. She reminded me that they agreed to play a role in helping you learn what you came here to learn. They agreed to teach us the hard lessons that ultimately shift our life. These lessons are what create the biggest and best "Ah ha" moments if we look for the possibility they bring. For me those people would be my mother, Jane (the women who kept me from moving to Asheville), and the minister at my father's funeral. They all reminded me that what I needed was already inside of me. In their own way they each forced me to go within and find my truth wrapped in possibility.

I hold no ill will for any messengers. They had big shoes to fill and I am grateful they kept their contract with me and it doesn't end there because I was a messenger for each of them. I brought each one of them a lesson or experience they came here to learn as well. We all kept our divine appointment and delivered what we agreed upon. I was a part of their plan and journey and they were a part of mine. There is no escaping it, we are all connected. We are all part of the same divinely woven matrix called quantum possibility. Every person and every event is part of the "All" playing itself out in accordance to the experiences we decided to have before we showed up in the physical form we call a body.

When I started to look at life and the people in my life this way, I began to understand that everything that has happened has been a gift, and every person an amazing messenger. I also know that not every teacher has a hard lesson. There are the light bringers and the cheerleaders who pick you up when you're down. There's Aunt Rose who has always been a beacon of perpetual light, gently helping me stay on my path, and without Greg and his message I never would have received hers. At the picnic, if Charlotte and Susan had not called me over to sit down I would never have met my moonbeam, Andrea. Andrea reminds me every day that possibility is everywhere and that dreams do come true. She has filled my life with love and given me every detail I wrote down and a few I never even thought of.

I can even see Linda, my stepmother in a positive way, and I better understand her role in my life. She reminds me that people can change and we need to allow them to do so. It is never too late because there is good in everyone; you just have to give them time to show you. It's important to remember these messengers and honor their purpose even though it's not always easy, these messengers are the ambassadors of the change you seek in your life.

I have also begun to understand the beauty of family and its message. Family lets you know you're okay, that you fit in and are connected, even if you have been gone for years. Yes, they do have the ability to rock you to your core but that's what good messengers do. They show you varying paths and then give you light and support to walk down your chosen path like my cousin did for me on the phone before the funeral, and again when she gathered all my aunts and cousins while giving me a safe haven to speak my truth.

It doesn't stop with people either; the journey is also about the events that lead you to one place or another.

Had I not gone to school and studied alternative medicine, I would have never understood that real healing is more about changing your thoughts than taking a pill. If I had not gone to school I would have never started publishing my online magazine or writing this book and yet when I arrived at school I had no idea this is where it would lead. Oh yeah, I forgot to tell you that part.

After going to school I couldn't decide what to do because it's not legal in most states to practice alternative medicine. So I decided to Consciously Shift that and created an online magazine where new ideas could take root for our changing world. I created a platform where all the people I knew could come and learn or teach about how to consciously shift life by giving information that informs and creates possibility. So even though school was a struggle and I didn't hear half of it, I still found possibility around the next corner. I thought I was going to be a naturopathic doctor and instead I'm a publisher. I once thought I would be a fighter pilot, soar about the clouds, and instead I got something better. I got me. I found my journey and I am living in my possibility.

All of these life experiences and people are the connections that take us from one place to another. Most of the time we brush them off as chance or we get so stuck in a situation we don't see the magic of the experience or the message unfolding right in front of us.

Make it a point to embrace the magic and honor the connections, events and messengers. They are not chance. They are the journey we chose before we came here, reminding us of who we are while showing us our possibility.

Scientists view these events as a phenomena called "Quantum Entanglement." Quantum Entanglement simply means it is all connected and it's all the same even though it looks or acts differently. I like to call it "Quantum Possibility" because you never know what great new conscious and shifting adventure your connection of possibility will bring. Always remember it's never too late to venture

down
    the
        rabbit
            hole
                of
                    possibility.

Chapter Seventeen

Possibility Tool Box

It has been two years since I decided to write my story of possibility. When I started the journey I had no idea what an adventure it would be. I was not prepared for the difficult and joyful rollercoaster of emotions that would show up to guide me through the writing and healing process. But I made it through even though I wasn't always sure I would. Yes, it was hard, but it has been worth it. Every day I feel more connected to me. Every day I see and feel more purpose. Every day I am happy I am alive and experiencing days that are both challenging and joyful.

It's not always easy. It takes work, patience, and it takes time. I know those are not things we want to hear, especially when we live in a world that believes all issues can be solved with a pill or in the time it takes to watch a sitcom.

Just be easy with you and know you can do it because you are the foremost expert on you, that everything that has happened, happened for a reason, and that you are the possibility you seek.

Below you will find some of the tools that helped me find my possibility. It is my hope that they can help you navigate your rabbit hole of possibility.

**It is important to note that these tips and tools are not meant to replace medical assistance when needed.

POSSIBILITY TOOLS

Breathing

> *"Feelings come and go like clouds in a windy sky. Conscious breathing is my anchor."*
>
> — *Thich Nhat Hanh, Stepping into Freedom: Rules of Monastic Practice for Novices*

Breathing is the most important tool on this list. It is also the most overlooked tool on this list. Breathing is everything and not just because you need oxygen to live.

Breathing increases blood flow in your body and more importantly it increases the blood flow to the brain. When our brain receives the optimum amount of blood we function and think more clearly and calmly. When we breathe deeply and purposefully we feel stronger, more grounded and are able to face daily stressors and challenges more easily.

Deep breathing and breathing exercises are the fastest and easiest way to calm a stressful moment and to improve health. When you take a moment to breathe deeply you stop everything and just focus on what's going on with you and your body. Deep breathing requires you to stop and go within and that's a good thing, because if you do not go within you will surely go without.

Write it Down

This seems so silly that I thought no way, that's just not going to work. Once I wrote things down though, they started to appear. Things like money, happiness and my moonbeam. Remember in Chapter 13 how I began to get clear about what I wanted for my life? I outlined exactly what I wanted in a life partner and more. Within just months it showed up and after seven years it keeps getting better.

Simply Google the words below for tips on how to get started:

Write It Down
Healing from Writing It Down
Healing Writing Exercises

Reading

> "I've never known any trouble than an
> hour's reading didn't assuage."
> ~Arthur Schopenhauer

Reading is an amazing healing tool depending on what you choose to read. My personal choices for transformation and healing are books that discuss positive and inspirational ideas. As mentioned in Chapter 12, books on laws of attraction really resonated with my soul and shined a light on my path. In addition to laws of attraction books, I have read and continue to read books about shamanic practices, energy healing, mind-body connection, self-healing, alternative medicine, nutrition, quantum physics and more.

The key here is to feed your mind with things that will uplift and open you to new ways of thinking and seeing life's challenges. You have to feed your heart and your soul with substance. There is no way you can address the same issue the same way every day and expect a different answer or result to appear.

Nutrition

"Tell me what you eat, and I will tell you
who you are."
~Jean Anthelme Brillat-Savarin

Nutrition and food are big topics these days. It is an industry driven by the sole purpose of getting your money.

There is so much misinformation out there that it's nearly impossible to know what is the best thing to eat, not to mention how to read a food label. It's very confusing and I by no means want to give you the idea that I understand it any better than the next person. But what I do know for sure is that what you eat you become. If you eat to bury emotions, you will continue to carry the weight of your burden and most likely you will expand. If you eat to sustain and build a healthy life, you will be stronger and healthier. Purpose is everything with food.

Below I have listed some ideas about food and what I did to lose the emotional fat I carried for years.

My basic rule of thumb with food is to eat whole foods that you have to actually cook. Organic meats and certain fruits and veggies are a must.

Meats- When it comes to meats, organic is the only way to go in my opinion. Animals have a closer cell structure to humans than plants. When you eat meat your body stores some of the fat present in the meat you eat. You don't want to store fat of genetically modified or chemical treated animals or the food they produce.

Veggies- Look online for lists of fruits and vegetables that do not have to be organic.

They are called the *dirty dozen* and the *clean fifteen*. Make it a point to eat local and seasonal produce. I know this is a bit hard because of the way we live in the world today, however just be informed. It will allow you to choose what is best for you.

You can heal your body with your food if you eat healing food.

> "Let food be thy medicine and medicine be thy food."
>
> — **Hippocrates**

Exercise
Exercise is great for raising your heart rate and breathing. As I mentioned in the first tool on this list, breathing is everything so exercise is a good complement to breathing healthier and increasing that blood flow.

Just be sure you are not replacing exercise with those few moments a day when you stop and breathe deeply. Remember those moments are like your daily check-in and they solidify your balance and align you with your purpose.

It's important to remember that exercise is about movement and strengthening. I won't lie to you. It's not always my strong suit and when I neglect or ignore my body I usually suffer. It is for this reason I make it a point to do activities that feed my body and speak to my soul, that way I am keeping balance and enjoying the journey.

Here are a couple of my favorite activities:

Yoga is awesome and there are so many versions out there today. I love yoga. It really resonates with my soul. I find that I can do a few yoga moves a day in my home and I'm aligned. I have been to several yoga centers and practice at home. Do what works for you.

As much as I love yoga I love walking even more. I love to commune with the trees in my city downtown and feel the energy of the bay. Walking lightens my heart and fills my soul with joy.

Another exercise I enjoy is Chi Gong. It's great for getting the blood flowing and helps with balance.

Meditation

Of everything in my toolbox this one is most valuable to me. I meditate every day without fail. Meditation is the morning ritual that sets up my whole day.

When I first started meditating it was hard because I had so much mind chatter. My mind chatter at that time was filled with fear. "What if I can't ____?" or "What if ____ happens?" and on and on.

When I first started to really focus on meditation it was hard, but I didn't give up. I had read too many things about how powerful it could be for stepping into possibility.

After some practice, meditation became my safe place and got me through some of the hardest times in my life. Remember Chapters 12 and 13. Thank goodness for meditation because that was what got me through.

There are as many ways to meditate, as there are leaves on trees. Find what works for you and do that.

These are just a few of the things I did to consciously shift my life into possibility. Most of the information I found was on the Internet. If you take the time to Google any one of the tools I mentioned here, you will find a never ending list of ideas and options. It's important to note that I did not pay for anything. I mention this only to reassure you that you do not need money to implement these tools. The information is out there on social media, web sites, and in blogs galore. Just find what resonates with you and use it until you are done and then find more. Remember things in life change often so it's better to be flexible and to show up with a full toolbox filled especially for you and by you.

Good Luck and Happy Conscious Shifting.

Chapter Eighteen

The Invitation

A special thank you to Oriah Mountain Dreamer for allowing the use of her poem *The Invitation*. Thank you Oriah for gifting the world with a literary compass that points in the direction of possibility when our vision is unclear.

The Invitation by Oriah

It doesn't interest me
what you do for a living.
I want to know
what you ache for
and if you dare to dream
of meeting your heart's longing.
It doesn't interest me
how old you are.
I want to know
if you will risk
looking like a fool
for love

for your dream
for the adventure of being alive.
It doesn't interest me
what planets are
squaring your moon...
I want to know
if you have touched
the centre of your own sorrow
if you have been opened
by life's betrayals
or have become shriveled and closed
from fear of further pain.
I want to know
if you can sit with pain
mine or your own
without moving to hide it
or fade it
or fix it.

I want to know
if you can be with joy
mine or your own
if you can dance with wildness
and let the ecstasy fill you
to the tips of your fingers and toes
without cautioning us
to be careful
to be realistic
to remember the limitations

of being human.
It doesn't interest me
if the story you are telling me
is true.
I want to know if you can
disappoint another
to be true to yourself.
If you can bear
the accusation of betrayal
and not betray your own soul.
If you can be faithless
and therefore trustworthy.

I want to know if you can see Beauty
even when it is not pretty
every day.
And if you can source your own life
from its presence.
I want to know
if you can live with failure
yours and mine
and still stand at the edge of the lake
and shout to the silver of the full moon,
"Yes."
It doesn't interest me
to know where you live
or how much money you have.
I want to know if you can get up
after the night of grief and despair

weary and bruised to the bone
and do what needs to be done
to feed the children.
It doesn't interest me
who you know
or how you came to be here.
I want to know if you will stand
in the centre of the fire
with me
and not shrink back.
It doesn't interest me
where or what or with whom
you have studied.
I want to know
what sustains you
from the inside
when all else falls away.
I want to know
if you can be alone
with yourself
and if you truly like
the company you keep
in the empty moments.

By Oriah © Mountain Dreaming,
from the book The Invitation
published by HarperONE, San Francisco,
1999 All rights reserved

Bibliography

Hicks, J. and E. (2006). The Law of Attraction: The Basics of the Teachings. California: Hay House, Inc.

About The Author

 Tracey R. Kern is the publisher of *Conscious Shift Magazine*, an on-line publication designed to explore mindful living and encourage readers to venture into quantum possibility whenever possible. She is a student of alternative medicine, a Reiki Master, Shamanic Practitioner, member of the monastery, energy healer and sought-after publisher. Today Tracey is living her happily ever after life with her wife Andrea, and their four-legged children, Neo and Jasmine.

To learn more about Tracey or *Conscious Shift Magazine*, visit

www.consciousshiftmagazine.com.